THE ACCIDENTAL BAKER

a cake for every crisis

Memoir

Barbara J Miachika

THE ACCIDENTAL BAKER

a cake for every crisis

Barbara J Miachika

NDYGIRLS PUBLISHING
POINCIANA, FLORIDA

ISBN: 0615787630
ISBN- 13: 978-0615787633

Library of Congress Control Number: 2013935747
NDYGIRLS Publishing
Poinciana, Florida

In Memory of Anton

For Anthony and Victoria, Paul and Julie, David and Sharon

and

Mike

Contents

My First Life

My Second Life

My Third Life

THE ACCIDENTAL BAKER

My introduction for success with baking.
Read before beginning this book.

Any book featuring baking usually adds a note regarding how to begin. My advice is…read the recipe through to the final presentation. This gives a visual and sets the scene. If you do this, there won't be a last minute rush to get missing ingredients or the correct cooking utensil. I give a hint of **Easy, Medium, or More Difficult** at the top of ingredients regarding the technique and ease of preparation.

A set of measuring spoons, cups, and a weight scale are a must.
A thermometer for meat and chocolate, bread making and candy are helpful.
Some of the recipes are simple, but many are advanced with chef's professional tips and techniques, producing wonderful results.
I am including directions for success with chocolate.

Measuring
My recipes use pounds, ounces, cups, tsp, Tbsp, qts.
Large eggs, unsalted butter.
Measuring cocoa, confectioner's sugar and flour, and most dry ingredients can be scooped, then leveled with a straight spatula.
Chocolate, nuts etc. when chopped should be weighed on a scale otherwise cup measurements will not be accurate.

Chocolate
Regarding the quality of chocolate mentioned in these recipes; coating chocolate is not correct for most recipes as it is not real chocolate.
Unsweetened, Baker's, Hershey's, Nestlé,
Dark Chocolate Bittersweet, Ghirardelli, Lindt Excellence, Callebaut.
Semisweet, Ghirardelli, Hershey's Baker's, Nestlé.
Semisweet Chocolate Chips, Baker's, Hershey's Nestlé, Ghirardelli.

Sweet Chocolate, Baker's, German Sweet Chocolate,
Swiss Milk, Lindt Swiss Milk.
Milk chocolate Chips, Baker's Hershey's, and Nestlé.
White Chocolate, Baker's Premium White Chocolate Baking Squares.
Lindt.
White Chocolate Chips, Hershey's, Nestlé.

Couverture is not a brand or type but a term used to describe the percentage of cocoa butter-at least 32 but as high as 39 percent for good quality. The extra cocoa butter allows for a thin shell for coating candies sometimes described as a crisp finish.
Cacao Barry, Lindt or Valrhôna.
For quantity, most brands can be purchased in 5 lb. slabs.

Working with Chocolate
Melting chocolate to use as a baking ingredient for candy work or decoration requires gentle heat. Chocolate that is overheated may scorch. Stir dark chocolates over hot not boiling water, several times as it begins to melt.
White and Milk Chocolate are more difficult because of the milk solids aversion to heat, and should be stirred constantly, melting over warm water, very low heat.
A double boiler, Pyrex insert on top or pot with a metal bowl fitting on top is easier.
Add coarsely chopped chocolate to bowl, over hot not boiling water. If overheated, chocolate can become grainy.
Melt, stirring until mostly smooth, set aside from pot and finish melting. Make sure to dry bottom of bowl with tea towel from any condensation.
Tempering; melting chopped chocolate over DB to 113 degrees, remove bowl, wipe bowl bottom to prevent drips into mixture, pour ½ out on to marble or cool counter. Spade back and forth to cool to

82 degrees. Scrape this chocolate back into the DB and bring all up to 89 degrees. It is now ready to use and won't turn grey when firm. Hold at this temperature if making fans or decorations. Then let decorations or coatings firm up in fridge once completed.

Many new blends of new chocolate are available for you to test. Just read the ingredients for information.

<u>Recipes</u>
Use recipe method as shown. Try not to substitute ingredients if not sure of results.
Sometimes a mixture needs to chill, (butter creams, or proof- yeast), even overnight, so plan ahead, read through to the end.
Pre-heat oven.
Baking is accurate, <u>not</u> like whipping up an entrée where anything goes.
Parchment paper and pastry bags with several tips are also additional tools.
All these recipes have been used many times. Most can be doubled or more, but be mindful of the spices or flavoring quantities; that might be a different ratio in quantity.

Enjoy the thrill of baking, creating something made with your love.

Preamble
Was I a Pastry Chef before?
1940

During World War 11 when sugar rationing was still in effect, my mother allowed me to use the entire month's portion of sugar coupons to create an irresistible confection that was pictured in a ladies magazine. I can still hear myself whining, "Please let me make that dessert, it looks so yummy." I was eight years old.

The recipe described two layers of buttery cake called a Genoise, a word I didn't know. "It's a type of sponge cake," my mother said. "The center is filled with ice-cream, and after re-freezing, the top is covered with towering clouds of fluffy meringue, that would need to be put under the tricky broil element in our oven." We did have a broil setting in our stove to do it. The Sunbeam Mixer that the article suggested was another modern piece of equipment that we had, (it seemed like every modern kitchen had at least a Sunbeam Mixer.) So I was all set.

My mother and I made a special trip to the nearest pharmacy for baking powder of medicinal quality suggested in the recipe, (I'm not sure why it was different), and later, she let me set out the ingredients, pans, mixer and bowl, and bake it all by myself. It seemed so natural. Maybe I had baked before?"

BAKED ALASKA

This is the recipe that started it all, my first exciting plunge into the art of pastries. I remember it was such a banner day because I was able to lick all the gooey meringue off the spoon and no one said, NO! I was in charge.

Prep time, start one day before cake is needed.
One 1x17 sheet pan for baking cake.
Easy

1 quart of chocolate ice cream
1 quart coffee ice cream
Sponge cake, see below
2 cups strawberries, sliced
Meringue, see below
Warm glossy chocolate sauce, see below

Sponge Cake or one plain yellow cake mix
10 eggs, separated, save whites
2 cups vegetable oil
4 cups sugar
Vanilla extract, to taste
6 cups flour
2 Tbsp. baking powder
2 cups milk

Meringue
1 cup egg whites, room temperature
1 cup sugar

Glossy Chocolate Sauce
3 oz. unsweetened chocolate
7 oz. semi-sweet chocolate
⅜ cup light corn syrup
½ cup hot water

Method
Preheat oven to only 325. In bowl of electric mixer, beat egg yolks, vegetable oil, and sugar until light. Add vanilla. Sift flour, baking powder.
Add in three additions alternately with milk.
Pour batter in greased, parchment lined pan.
Bake 25-30 minutes.
When cool invert onto parchment, halve the cake, horizontally.
Place a 2 qt. stainless bowl, on ½ cake. Cut this cake for the base, the one you are going to use to make an ice-cream dome,
Set aside. Save scraps for trifle or other uses.
Turn bowl over, cover inside of stainless bowl with plastic wrap, up and over edges
Spoon ½ of softened strawberry ice cream into bowl.
Add strawberries.
Spoon ½ of softened chocolate ice cream over berries.
Press down to level surface.
Add one more layer of each or nearly up to top of bowl.
Place cake circle on top, pressing down to match top of bowl.
Freeze several hours or overnight.

Pre heat oven to 500, a hot oven, and position racks at lowest level.

In an electric mixer, whisk whites to soft peaks.
Slowly add sugar while continually whisking.

Meringue should be stiff.
Remove frozen dome from freezer.
Use a cookie sheet, place a piece of parchment on it, invert bowl with frozen cake onto parchment.
The cake part is now the base.
Lift off bowl, remove plastic wrap.
Encase rounded form including cake with meringue. Freeze several hours or overnight.
Bake from freezer, 2-3 or 4 minutes to lightly brown meringue.
Plate and serve in wedges.
Make chocolate sauce or use extra strawberries for a fresh coulis sauce of berries (Just
mash berries with 1Tbsp. sugar, chill.

My First Life

1

West Vancouver, 1974

I t happened with no warning, one sunny morning mid-week, as I stood whisking lemon pound cake ingredients.

He burst into the kitchen screaming "I'm no longer a partner, they voted me out!" Slamming his fist down on the butcher block counter, his face flaming with rage and disbelief, Anton seemed on fire.

Stunned, my questions spilled out onto the counters, "What's gone wrong at the dealership, what's happened to your partnership? How could they vote you out? You're the only professional person there. You're the comptroller, you're their Chartered Accountant. They need you."

I was talking about the Four Seasons Leisure World and the Mercury/Lincoln Dealership in North Vancouver, of which he was a one-third partner. Cars and sports-equipment was a great money-maker. We were getting used to lots of perks that went with this kind of business; memberships in all the golf and tennis clubs, a bottom-less line of credit in the sports department of Leisure World, and a variety of new cars. Money was almost no object. Everything came out of stock.

He needed to tell me more but his ego got in the way. In the next instant, he sputtered, took a deep breath and said "I'll be up at the club." He was out the door, before I could catch my breath. The Capilano Golf and Country Club was his easy haven just up the street.

I had been mixing pound cakes for the school bake sale. A shroud of worry niggled my mind for what might be ahead. I tried to shake it, putting such disturbing thoughts aside. The dust settled. I stood frozen in space, his words falling over me like a heavy woolen cloak, tipping me off balance. I was confused, paralyzed, and light-headed for the moment, my mind blank. I had never seen my husband like this, so wild, out of control. My fingers grasped the butcher block counter for support. Sunlight fell in patterns across my counters from the skylight above that stretched thirty feet across the vaulted roof line. My safe world was still here, but everything had changed. For the first time I imagined the worst.

As I look back, I knew I could no longer deceive myself that ours was a perfect marriage; loving, carefree and without tears. A bumpy road here and there was to be expected. I told myself, "That's what real life is about."

He was a difficult, demanding man. Anton wanted the best for himself, for me and our three sons. He was so hard on the boys if they slipped up anywhere. Coiling the garden hose just so on the patio or on the sailboat deck was the thing, everything had to be tidy and ship-shape. I can still see the boys rolling their eyes as their father chewed them out to do it right. It was these small things that drove Anton crazy. It was his nature to be organized.

He came from a strong immigrant family determined to better themselves. My husband was the first in his family to obtain a university degree. His choice was chartered accountancy, C.A. in Canada, but described in the states as a C.P.A.

Anton always encouraged me to reach for the top in any of my endeavors; with the household, cooking, in sports or with our boys. From the beginning, a firm, manly handshake from our boys was a must when being introduced to our friends or guests. We set the bar high. As a family we were each confident in our daily routines.

The cakes I had been mixing momentarily stalled, the batter falling to the bottom of the bowl. I inhaled a deep breath, the pungent aroma of lemon zest drifted over me, bringing me back to my immediate task. I pulled myself together; wiped my hands on my apron, re-mixed the cakes and spooned the smooth, golden batter into the greased pans, sliding them into my new Wolf, gas oven.

LEMON POPPY SEED POUND CAKE

Every baker needs at least one good pound cake recipe. This one can be doubled and different flavors like orange or coconut essence are easily substituted.
Note, this cake is perfect for any occasion.
It adds a note of nostalgia and goodness to any meal.

Easy
Serves 12
Oven 350, 1 hour, 10 minutes
Loaf pan, parchment

1 cup unsalted butter
3 cups cake flour
2 cups sugar
1¾ tsp. baking powder
¼ tsp. baking soda
½ tsp. salt
4 large eggs, separated
1Tbsp. Poppy seeds
Zest of 3 lemons
½ cup lemon juice
2Tbsp. sugar
1 cup low fat buttermilk

Method
Preheat oven, grease loaf pan, line with parchment.
Sift together flour, baking powder, baking soda, poppy seeds, and salt.

In bowl of mixer, cream butter. Gradually add 2 cups sugar, beating 2 minutes to blend well.
Add egg yolks, add lemon zest.
Whisk whites to soft peaks; fold into butter/sugar, egg mixture.
Begin and end with flour, incorporate flour mixture with buttermilk. Beat lightly to combine.
Spread batter in loaf pan.
Bake in lower ⅓ of oven about 1 hour 10 minutes or until a tooth pick comes out clean and cake is nicely browned on top. While still warm, drizzle on glaze. Cool in pan on rack.

Glaze

1Tbsp. lemon juice 1 cup icing sugar. Pour over warm loaf and enjoy.

2
Baking and Desserts

With the cakes wrapped and ready for the bake sale, I began production on our own dessert for dinner that night. I decided on Nouvelle Crème Brûlée.

When confronted with any crisis, I baked. When something deep inside me wanted to set things right, baking was my solution, giving me a tangible to hold onto for the moment.

Small round dessert molds came out of the new glass cupboards. Sliding my fingers over the smooth ceramic shapes, I could already taste the results ahead. The velvety smooth baked custard so carefully timed, rested under a sugar coated crusty baguette slice. The bread was grilled to a caramelized crunchiness to create my version of Crème Brûlée. When I served it, I would add a dollop of whipped cream on top and raspberry coulis as a finishing touch around the edges.

Wiping away the devastating encounter with Anton, earlier that morning, I reassured myself, "At least I'll have a sweet finish to our day." I was almost back at my comfort level. I still had a lot to learn about life.

BARBARA'S NOUVELLE CRÈME BRÛLÉE

This recipe is more delicious than regular Crème Brûlée because the addition of a small crusty slice of baguette on the custard surface, buttered and encrusted with crunchy sugar adds more taste and texture. Raspberry or blueberry sauce is a perfect balance. I like raspberry best.

Oven 350
30 minutes
Water bath
Serves 8
Medium

8 French bread slices ¼ thick
2 whole eggs
5 egg yolks
¼ cup granulated sugar
½ tsp vanilla
Nutmeg, fresh grated
2 cups milk
2 cups heavy cream
Crushed sugar cubes for the buttered surface of baguette
Dusting of icing sugar

Method
Butter bread on one side, press into crushed sugar.
Heat milk, cream and ¼ cup granulated sugar until scalded.
Whisk egg yolks and whole eggs, add hot cream slowly to eggs, whisking constantly.
Sieve egg/milk mixture into 8 small custard cups, (6oz size).

Place bread on top, sugar side up.
Bake custards in water bath until tests done, about 30 minutes.
Serve warm or cold, with a dollop of whipped cream on top, with fruit sauce or plain.

3

Homemaker

I loved being a homemaker, and never wanted to be the bread winner like some career women in the '60's. I was traditional for my times; my children and home were my career, my everything. Keeping a well-stocked pantry, daily clean-ups, vacuuming and dusting were not chores but fun for me and thoroughly satisfying.

With all the daily activities, food was still one of the most important parts of my life. It bound us together as a family, not to just exist but was truly an art form for me. We were part of the new 'Foodies' eating fish and Mediterranean foods not yet popular in the markets. My interest in everything culinary was voracious. Before long I mastered boning out the 20 pound salmon brought home from Anton's father's boat, the 'Beachy Head'. Cleaning slippery squid from Vancouver's exotic Chinatown was another gutsy talent I developed.

Granville Market, a wildly successful food market under the Granville Bridge at False Creek, in the center of the city, held a plethora of everything I needed. A Saturday morning excursion over the Lion's Gate Bridge to the market was an inspiring way to start the day. After I wedged my car into an impossibly small parking space,

I clutched my purse, a canvass catch-all for my groceries and ventured forth. I never consciously shopped for price; as Anton's wife I didn't need to. It was all about freshness and quality. That's what I wanted.

At the market entrance, the flower stalls assaulted my senses, making it impossible not to stand and enjoy the spectacle. Breathing in the staggering beauty of hydrangeas, lilies and freesia, the selection was dizzying. I spied the roses I had hoped for. There were dozens of delicate, dewy pink roses, waiting since four AM for today's buyers, waiting for me to use on a friend's birthday cake. Pointing, I just smiled my choice at the flower vendor and he acknowledged me. He set aside the perfect ones. I continued shopping. My first item was crossed off the list.

Aromas wafting out from the crusty artisan breads and morning pastries were enough to sway me out of any diet idea I had that day. I waited in line. "I'll have two croissants, two of those crusty breads, and two yummy breakfast jam tarts," I said, signaling my choices to the salesgirl over the other buyers around me. I carefully tucked my purchases into my bag. Out on the front dock, facing the water of False Creek, I sat on one of the resting stools and ate a croissant before continuing any further.

Strolling inside again, I discovered fresh, pink-speckled prawns still wiggling on top of their icy bed. Unable to resist, I decided right then what our family would have for dinner tonight. I promptly bought three pounds of them. An excellent recipe for prawns was already in my mind. It was hard to pass up the impressive displays of stinky cheeses, ripe berries and bunches of baby carrots, with their delicate roots and leafy, green, earthy tops still intact. But I did have a big list to fill so I pressed on.

Stopping at the bell peppers, I said to the vendor, "Please give me four red and four yellow peppers and include that leafy head of cabbage over there." I was planning to make 'Sarma," during the week, a Yugoslavian specialty for a family get-together.

'Sarma' is composed of cabbage leaves filled and rolled like fat, glistening cigars. The presentation can also include whole red and yellow bell peppers using the same filling. Cabbage and peppers are stuffed with varying mixtures of rice, ground pork, bacon, garlic and seasonings. Whole, smoked pork jowls can be added in the center of the pot giving a rustic, elusive, smoky intensity. Just try this recipe and you will be hailed a winner.

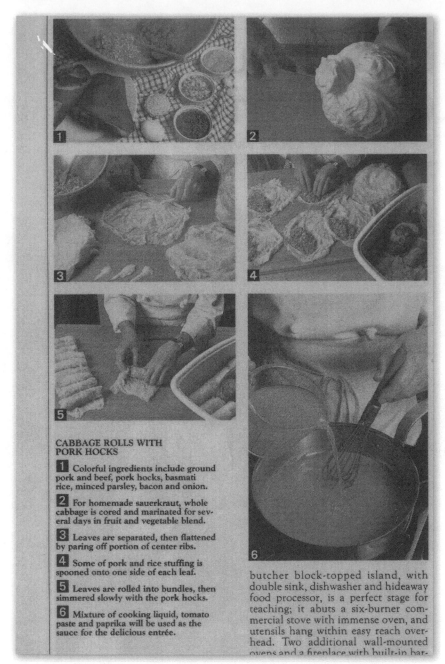

CABBAGE ROLLS WITH PORK HOCKS

1 Colorful ingredients include ground pork and beef, pork hocks, basmati rice, minced parsley, bacon and onion.

2 For homemade sauerkraut, whole cabbage is cored and marinated for several days in fruit and vegetable blend.

3 Leaves are separated, then flattened by paring off portion of center ribs.

4 Some of pork and rice stuffing is spooned onto one side of each leaf.

5 Leaves are rolled into bundles, then simmered slowly with the pork hocks.

6 Mixture of cooking liquid, tomato paste and paprika will be used as the sauce for the delicious entrée.

butcher block-topped island, with double sink, dishwasher and hideaway food processor, is a perfect stage for teaching; it abuts a six-burner commercial stove with immense oven, and utensils hang within easy reach overhead. Two additional wall-mounted ovens and a fireplace with built-in bar-

The Bon Appétit photo-shoot of Barbara preparing Cabbage Rolls and Stuffed Peppers

SARMA

This is one of the Yugoslavian specialties I produced for the "Robust Cuisine of Yugoslavia," Bon Appétit's Magazine article in 1986, featuring ten pages of script and pictures. Now I would be crowned the queen of all things Yugoslavian.

Serves 8
1½ -2 hours
Medium

1 large onion, cut into pieces
2 oz. bacon
¼ cup minced parsley
2 garlic cloves
½ lb. lean pork
½ lb. ground beef
¼ cup basmati rice
1 egg
S/P
1 large head of cabbage, blanched
2 pork hocks or some smoked spare ribs
2 whole garlic heads
2Tbsp. flour
1Tbsp. tomato paste
1½ tsp. Hungarian paprika
Fresh chervil

Method
Use a large stock pot with enough boiling water to cover cabbage.

Blanch to make leaves pliable.

Remove and drain.

When cool enough to handle, separate leaves, trying not to tear leaves.

Cut off thick part of spine at base of leaf using a small knife.

Process onion, bacon, meats, parsley and 2 garlic cloves to lightly blend.

Place in a medium bowl; add egg, rice and s/p.

Spread each leaf flat and spoon about 1-2 tb filling through center area, leaving edges free.

Roll up from bottom, thick end; fold in sides as you go, ending at the thin edge of leaf.

Place seam side down on counter. Continue with all available leaves.

Chop any broken or small leaves and place in bottom of baking casserole or Dutch oven.

Place pork hocks in middle of the pot, add rolls seam side down around pork.

Pour enough cold water to just cover rolls.

Bring to a boil, reduce heat and simmer, covered until meats are cooked and rice is tender, about 1 ½ hours.

Meanwhile, preheat oven to 350, arrange garlic heads, tops cut to expose cloves, on foil or dish, and drizzle with olive oil. Roast 1 hour. Set aside.

Skim fat from cooking liquid. Leave liquid and rolls in pot.

Put skimmed fat into small sauce pan, whisk in flour, tomato paste and seasonings.

Cook 2 minutes to make a nice flavouring for sauce.

If it is too thin, make beurre manie, (an equal flour/butter combination mixed to a paste,) stir in 1tb. at a time, and simmer to correct texture.

Stir liquid, covering rolls in main pot, simmer briefly.
Lift rolls onto a warm platter putting pork hocks or spare ribs in center.
Add whole roasted garlic on top, placing cabbage rolls around meats; serve cooking liquid, skimmed of any fat, in sauce boat.
Accompany with mashed potatoes if desired.

Note, canned, drained sauerkraut can be added to the pot bottom before placing cabbage rolls around the hocks.

4
Chefs

My collection of hastily torn out recipes from doctor's waiting rooms or hurried scribblings written on a napkin at a restaurant, piqued my eyes, nose and palate. I could visualize, smell and taste each combination in my mind. Every opportunity to try something new jumped out at me, especially chocolate. Every day was dessert day for me. It was all too wonderful.

Shiny pictures in food magazines were starting to show those fabulous close-up shots so hard to resist. Gourmet and Bon Appétit in particular were first to know how to make you buy the current issue. I'd muse, "Why didn't I think of using chocolate like that? I will experiment tomorrow." Often my girlfriends made arrangements to meet for lunch, but I stayed at home and baked desserts.

On my kitchen shelf I had *"Mastering the Art of French Cooking"* by Julia Child, *"La Technique"* and *"La Method,"* by Jacques Pépin and *"The Classic Italian Cookbook,"* by Marcella Hazan. The commercial magazines, plus the above tomes stirred some of my first inspirations, especially those of Jacques Pépin, whom I declared my forever mentor.

CHOCOLATE IMPERIALÉ FLOURLESS CAKE

This is a special dark chocolate single layer cake, very dense and glazed with a shiny ganache. It is an impressive centerpiece for a sit down dinner and is best made ahead to mellow. Hold in the fridge; bring to room temperature to serve. I think Jacques gave me this recipe. Every restaurant now tries to make this cake! I have doubled it with success and added clustered chocolate fans on the top for pizazz.

Serves 10
9"spring form pan
Oven 375
Medium

4 oz. semi-sweet chocolate, chopped
4 oz. unsalted butter
⅔ cup sugar
Zest of 1 orange
1 Tbsp. Grand Marnier liqueur
3 eggs
6 oz. walnuts, ground, (approx. 2 cups) can be part hazelnuts, almonds.

Method
Preheat oven to 375. Position a rack in middle of oven. Grease and flour 9"pan, also cut a parchment circle for bottom.
Melt chocolate and butter on low heat, over water bath. Add sugar while warm. Add orange zest.

Transfer to mixing bowl, add Grand Marnier.
Add eggs mixing in not beating.
Stir in nuts, (i.e. flour,). Pour into pan.
Bake at 375 until still fudgy but starting to dry at edges, about
25-30 minutes. Do not over bake. It will firm up some as it cools.
Remove to rack, cool in pan. Turn upside down on rack,
remove paper.
When completely cool, glaze.

Glaze
4 oz. semi-sweet chocolate
1 Tbsp. light corn syrup
2 oz. unsalted butter

8 whole hazel nuts to decorate edges
½ cup sugar for caramel

Method
Over hot not boiling water, melt chocolate and butter in a
stainless bowl.
Add corn syrup just before glazing cake.
Note. Fill any surface holes with thin coat of glaze first, i.e. A
crumb coat. Let cool.
Pour warm mixture over cake, from center outwards, tilting
cake to flow evenly.

Make sure to re warm glaze if needed.
Do the final finish.
Use any left-over glaze, put it in a paper cone with a fine tip
and write *Imperialé* on cake top.

5
Wine Making

As a young bride, and the first Canadian marriage in the Miachika domain, I was eager to fit into the world of my European in-laws, embracing all their traditions that are part of every Yugoslav household. I had no thoughts of disappointments, depression, tears or tough times. What could I know? I had said "for better or worse, richer or poorer," but no one ever expects worse and poorer.

Like a sponge, I was absorbing all these traditions that bored the young girls from the Slav families in Vancouver. They wanted modern, to be away from all the old world stuff. I melded so easily into this European setting, wanting to be everything to everyone. I was going to be the perfect daughter-in-law. Thinking back to a basic teaching moment for me, my mother-in-law stands front and center.

Mrs. Miachika Sr. was the self-taught wine expert. She passed on the old world knowledge of picking *gripes* at their peak of their intense, juicy, sugariness and flavor. "It is all in the fingers and the mouth," she said; pronouncing the words grapes, stickiness and tasting in her now quaint accent.

"Watch and see, this is how I will create our perfect vintage for the following winter." Again she showed me the sugar tricks, touch and taste, to unravel the mysteries of wine production. Now I could try. It was fun to carry on these old world customs. Homemade wine was part of all their traditional wedding and holiday celebrations; wine was always on the table next to a pitcher of cold water, to be mixed half and half in the glass. Everyone drank wine, even the children.

This ritual continued for many summers and I looked forward to it and the familial closeness that it created. This knowledge and many of my mother-in-law's personal recipes, like the one following, were added to my cache of treasures. Anton's European family background gave me the know-how that would carry me forward when all else was gone.

CHOCOLATE ALMOND TORTA

This walnut Torta is a wonderful, moist cake and a standard in the Miachika repertoire. It is the familiar dessert made so many times that a recipe was never present. But here are the ingredients and method for you to follow until it becomes your favourite cake too!

Medium
Un-greased tube pan
Oven 350
Baking 50 minutes

Cake
8 oz. almonds skins on, lightly toasted
10 arrowroot cookies or vanilla wafers pulverized, about ⅔ cup
1oz, (1 square) semi-sweet chocolate

8 egg whites
1¼ cup sugar
1 tsp vanilla
2 Tbsp. brandy ½ tsp almond extract
8 drops of bitter almond extract, Oetker brand
Pinch of salt

Method
Pulverize almonds, cookies and chocolate in food processor, set aside.
Beat egg whites until they form soft peaks, gradually add ¼ cup sugar and beat to stiff peaks but not dry.

Beat egg yolks with 1 cup sugar until light and fluffy.
Add vanilla, almond extract, bitter almond brandy and salt.
Beat until very thick.
Fold in almond mixture with egg whites and yolk mixture.
Bake in un-greased tube pan approx. 50 minutes.
Invert to cool.

Walnut Icing
½ cup finely ground walnuts
1 Tbsp. sugar
¼ cup milk
1 Tbsp. chocolate almond liqueur
⅓ cup butter, soft
2 cups icing sugar
¼ cup chocolate almond liqueur

Method
Combine walnuts, sugar, and milk in small sauce pan.
Cook over low heat until thick, remove and cool.
Cream butter; add icing sugar and walnut mixture from above.
Beat to spreading consistency.
Slice cake in two.
Sprinkle liqueur on cut surfaces.
Spread cut surfaces with about 14 of the icing.
Put cake together, ice top and sides, garnish with chocolate curls.

BURGUNDY WINE MOLD

This jelled condiment is a nice accompaniment to a luncheon plate, a buffet or with roast chicken or pork. It has a surprising fresh flavor touched with black cherries. JELL-O was a very sixties image but still good today. A new way to use JELL-O

Serves 6
Easy

2 small boxes cherry Jell-O
1½ cups boiling water, (the normal amount would be two.)
2 cups cold Burgundy wine
1 (16 oz.) can pitted black cherries, cut into <u>fine</u> dice.
Almond essence, see below.
Rum or rum essence 1 tb, optional
1 cup heavy cream, whipped, garnish

<u>Method</u>
Dissolve Jell-O into boiling water, stir to dissolve. Add cold wine, then diced cherries. Soak in rum, optional.
Brush inside of terrine or fluted mold lightly with vegetable oil and/or drop of almond essence, (for fresh flavor).
Pour mixture into prepared mold.
Refrigerate until firm, about 4 hours or overnight.
Un-mold on decorative plate with raised edge.
Garnish with swirls of whipped cream or pile cream into side dish.

Chef

Note 1, reducing liquid by ½ cup of water gives a stiffer, perfect finish when unmolded.

Note 2, rinse the service plate with cold water. This allows the jelled dessert to move slightly in case you didn't get it centered at first placement.

6
Family dinners

S pecial dinners happened a lot, any occasion created the need. Birthdays were a big event. One pie or cake was never enough. Elaborate desserts were the highlight at the end of every get together. Zorka, Anton's young sister was caught up in our culinary world and brought something new to every get-together.

Magical Baron of Beef and Meringue Pie were two, such delights. Perfectly roasted baron of beef for the entrée and crisp, dry meringue with a soft spongy center, thick whipped cream and fresh sliced strawberries composed the dessert to finish the evening.

ROAST OF BEEF

Amazing but true!
Many times Anton and I or the boys would have
large parties and the roast beef was the center of
the buffet. Just bring it out on a platter, slice the
first slice and it will be the exact doneness all the
way through. Just like magic.

Any (rib bones or boneless) or top round of beef.

Mid-afternoon, start yourself about 4 hours resting, for serving around 6 pm. (This includes the final roasting time.)
Rub meat with garlic, dry mustard and soy sauce.
Season with salt and pepper no flour.
Place beef in roasting pan, uncovered, and turn oven to 375, roast for 1 hour.
Turn off oven, do not open door at all. <u>Do not peek!</u>

For rare roast beef 45 minutes before serving time, turn oven to 300.
For medium roast beef 50 minutes before serving time, turn oven to 300.
For well-done roast beef 55 minutes before serving time, turn oven to 300.

That's all, don't peek.

<u>Chef tip</u>, this works very well as long as you have more than one oven, or don't need the oven for any other part of your meal.

MERINGUE ANGEL PIE

This is a meringue dessert from the early years when the wives exchanged recipes trying to out-do each other. This is a great way to use leftover egg whites. This delicate and airy concoction is delicious and impressive.

Oven 250
Serves 6-8
Medium

6 egg whites
½ tsp. salt
1½ Tbsp. cornstarch
Pinch of cream of tartar
2 cups sugar
¼ cup fresh lemon juice
3 drops red food coloring (optional)
1 tsp. vanilla
½ tsp almond extract
1 cup fresh or frozen (thawed, drained) strawberries
2 cups heavy whipping cream, whipped (or lemon curd and sour cream)
Berries for the top

Method
Grease and flour a metal pie pan, bang out the excess. Set aside.
In a large mixer bowl, beat whites and salt on medium until foamy.

Increase speed; add 1 cup sugar 1 Tbsp. at a time. Whisk until sugar grains are dissolved and not grainy.

Add vanilla, lemon juice, and almond extract while slowly adding the last cup of sugar. Add food coloring.

Meringue will be stiff and glossy.

Mound meringue in pie shell spreading to edges but leaving center shaped like a dome.

Bake cake/meringue in lower ⅓ of oven at 250 for 1½ hours, then 300 for ½ hour.

<u>Make sure your oven low temperature reading is correct.</u>

Cool on counter, lift off cracked pieces, fill with whipped cream, strawberries, or optional, sour, replace cracked pieces, refrigerate. Let rest 3 hours or more. Cut as for pie.

Note, possible other fillings are: blueberries, raspberries, pineapple. Everyone was always amazed by this dessert.

7

West Vancouver House

In two years, Anton finished his chartered accountancy degree and promptly opened his own practice in a professional building in the center of Vancouver, expecting clients to find him. A brash move but so like him. He was young but had great business sense and soon was able to build up a varied group of needy customers wanting his services. He had a Midas touch, a winning way, bringing in new security every day.

In short order we outgrew our starter house in the Burnaby suburbs, and moved to a prestigious home in the British Properties, a very fashionable area of West Vancouver.

I had an image of what a perfect wife should look like. Before moving to our new home, I sewed three little cotton dresses to do everyday housework in. Red, green and blue, cotton gingham, each one had a gathered skirt and little puffed sleeves fitted with a small waist, to accent my slim figure, all very "Brady Bunch." I did all my own cleaning, windows, floors, baskets of laundry and ironed and starched his shirts.

BARBARA'S AMERICAN APPLE PIE

What a perfect pie to set out for dinner in our new house. The aroma of apple pie completed a homey feeling for kids and husband as we sat down together. Notice this is an oil based crust, very easy, no fail and very delicious. A handful of dried cranberries can be added to the filling.

Oven 425 30-45 minutes
Easy

Crust
1½ cups flour
2 tsp. sugar
1 tsp. salt
½ cup Canola oil (can also use Crisco)
2 Tbsp. milk

Method
Combine dry ingredients in processor.
Add oil (Crisco) and pulse.
Add milk.
Blend to crumbly stage.
Press into 9" pie tin. Use fingers to press into pan and crimp top edges/chill.

Filling
6 apples, peeled, cored and sliced
½ cup sugar
3 Tbsp. quick tapioca
½ tsp. cinnamon

1 tsp. nutmeg,
½ tsp. salt1 tsp. fresh lemon juice

Method
Mix all filling in a bowl except apples. Add apples and coat, mixing all.
Add to pie shell, mounding in center. Looks like a lot of filling but it will cook down some and be just right.

Pre-heat oven to 425

Crumble Topping
½ cup flour
¼ cup oatmeal
½ cup brown sugar
½ tsp. cinnamon
½ cup, (1stick) butter
Combine and pulse in processor only to crumbly stage.
Cover top of pie.
Place a flat bake sheet in oven under pie to catch any drips.
Bake 40 minutes, cover with foil to keep from browning too much, bake 5-10 minutes more.
Cool on rack. Serve plain or with whipped cream or Vanilla Ice Cream.

This is a very good and easy pie.

8
Chocolate Fantasies

Our family dessert competition continued with more berries, custards and chocolate in every sinfully wicked combination. Deep, dark semi-sweet chocolate, creamy milk chocolate, Belgian Gianduija, (a nut paste chocolate,) un-sweetened and pure white chocolate provided endless variations. I was always looking for a new way to use chocolate.

I was flexible, created themed dinners or fabulous parties with ease and became the perfect nurturer: a model woman of the fifties and sixties. I was good at everything in my domain. The early years were busy and I had the world by the tail.

Now I reminisce about us all, Anton's family members and me, sharing life, food and recipes. Years later when Anton died, in an indecorous mood the Miachika clan no longer spoke to or included me. They shunned me! Never spoke to me again! Mrs. Sr. was unable to accept that her perfect boy was not so perfect.

I was out, a knife in the back! After all these years, it was so false on their part, so condescending. I couldn't believe it! They blamed me. Damn them! I was allowing myself a moment of hurt and self- pity.

BEST EVER CHOCOLATE SHEET CAKE

Oven 350, bake 20 minutes
Spray or grease sheet pan 11x17 mark into 8x5= 35 squares

Easy

Cake
2 cups flour
2 cups granulated sugar
¼ tsp salt
4 heaping tb cocoa
2 sticks butter
1 cup boiling water
½ cup buttermilk
2 beaten eggs
1 tsp. baking soda
1 tsp. vanilla

Icing
1¾ sticks butter
4 Tbsp. heaping cocoa
6 Tbsp. milk
1 tsp. vanilla
1 lb. minus ½ cup powdered sugar

Method
In a mixing bowl combine flour, salt and granulated sugar.
In a saucepan, melt butter, stir in cocoa.
Add 1 cup boiling water to the cocoa mixture, allow to boil 30 seconds, Turn off heat.
Pour over flour mixture in bowl, stir to mix and cool slightly.

In small bowl, mix buttermilk, beaten eggs, baking soda and vanilla.

Add to chocolate/flour mixture. Mix thoroughly with spatula.

Pour onto sheet pan, bake in pre heated oven, middle rack, 18-20 minutes.

Icing

While cake is baking make icing.

Melt butter, stir in cocoa.

Turn off heat, add milk, vanilla and sieved powdered sugar. (See note for smooth icing).

Note---Strain icing through fine sieve into butter/cocoa mixture.

Remove cake from oven when done, let rest 5 minutes on cake rack to cool slightly, then pour icing over cake.

Leave undisturbed until almost cool. <u>Using a big knife, mark into squares only through icing, not all the way down. When the icing holds shape, finish cutting through cake. Wipe knife as you cut rows. This makes a nice finish without cracking icing.</u>

Optional top decoration, I use Hines store bought chocolate icing for this. Use a pastry bag with star tip to put finish rosette on each small square. Refrigerate until needed.

9

House Renovation

We had been married for twenty-two years and had done two small renos in our West Vancouver house before. We were a year and a half into this current, elaborate home renovation. It had really dragged on. I'd had enough of cooking breakfast outside in the dark on a two burner hot plate on the front patio, waiting for my kitchen to be finished. I felt worn down by it all. Walls were open to the north shore winter winds. Why had I agreed to this big mess? A fat mountain rat sneaking in under the temporary plastic partitions was caught in a trap the boys set up the night before. Ugh! Blood sploshed on the white, British India carpet!

"Help," I screamed, running down the hallway hoping one of the boys would cart the disgusting sight away and rescue me. It was all too much.

The costs kept mounting, thousands over the initial quote because Anton kept changing the specifications, enlarging the sauna, adding gold faucets and creating custom cabinetry touches everywhere; like the mirrored, box ceiling over the pool table that took a finishing carpenter two weeks to create. Money was no object.

I said, "Think of the cost of it all. The contractor loves it, the carpenter loves it. Are we sure we can pay for all this?" I was trying to be sensible.

I did trust but when I asked, he said "We can afford it, don't worry," Anton was the one in charge of our finances.

I muttered sarcastically, "You are the one with the golden touch."

BASIC SOURDOUGH STARTER AND BREAD

Fabulous homemade bread, crusty, chewy and real! Aromas drifting throughout the house while baking bread made everyone dizzy with desire. It is far cheaper to make your own loaves as well as obtaining wonderful flavor. The tops can be sprinkled with sesame seeds or try fennel seeds. Diced cheddar or tangy bits of Jalapeno pepper can also be interesting. This recipe was part of my bread class at Cuisine de Barbara.

Easy

Starter
4 whole potatoes, peeled, cut into chunks
3 pint of cold water
½ cup sugar
1 package of yeast, or 2½ tsp
1 cup lukewarm water

Method
This is the starter. Cook the potatoes in water, remove all to a bowl, mash and cool.
Mix warm water, yeast, and sugar in a small bowl. Let foam, then add potato mixture and yeast mixture together. Stand at room temperature for several days to develop and sour. This is your starter to keep in the refrigerator and draw from for future baking.
When removing starter, replace with some warm water and 1 tsp sugar. Place back in refrigerator.

Bread 5 Loaves
1 cup of starter from above
½ cup warm water with 1 tsp sugar
1 package yeast or 2½ tsp, or 1 fresh cube of yeast
3½ cups warm water or potato water
¼ cup veg. oil
¼ cup sugar
1½ Tbsp. salt, (add last)
6 cups all-purpose flour
5 more cups flour as needed for smooth, elastic dough
Cornmeal for sprayed bread pans

Method
Let starter come to room temperature, mix sugar/water, add yeast to foam.
Put water/oil/sugar/in large bowl.
Add enough flour to stir and make sticky dough.
Add salt now.
Add more flour, mixing with wooden spoon, then with fingers, stirring well from the bottom.
Turn out onto dusted counter, and knead to smooth, elastic ball about 10 minutes.
Heat oven to lowest setting, allow to warm briefly, then turn heat off.
Place dough in lightly oiled bowl, turn ball over to coat, cover bowl and place in warmed oven for 2 hours or double in bulk.
Punch down, turn out on counter and divide into 5 balls.
Let rest 10 minutes.
Roll out each ball into rectangle 9x15. Seal ends, shape into loaf, pinching seam and place into greased/cornmeal bread pans to rise in warm place. (About 30 minutes)

<u>Pre heat oven to 425</u>

Spray tops with water during baking for crusty finish. Bake about 40 minutes to brown well and sound hollow when tapped.

10

Creative Décor

I had lots of energy and needed some diversion from all the dust and wood shavings from the construction crew. It had gone on for months.

A weaving class held in a North Vancouver warehouse was advertised in the Lonsdale News, a local paper. A girlfriend had signed up and wanted company.

She said, "You would be good at this, lets' go together and see what its' about?"

I had never tried this art form before. Off-loom weaving, not standard patterns immediately grabbed my attention. Sketching a paper 'cartoon,' understanding how to set up the warp and woof, dying your own colours from hand spun wool. It was all quite challenging. So much to learn. I had bags of fluffy wool and textured yarns spilling from dozens of boxes and baskets in the garage and family room.

The carpenters working on our house renovation were coerced into hammering up a freestyle loom in a room designed to be a tool and wine storage space in the new garage.

They said, "Sure, we can do a little side job for you." They nailed up a frame between two existing studs. Two 10 foot two-by-fours were positioned top and bottom, eight feet high and three feet off the floor. Strong nails were hammered one inch apart down the faces of the lumber so I could create the stringing of warp and woof using my kitchen twine. How opportunistic to have the help of the workmen. My "cartoon vision" was to create ocean waves crested with foam, hitting the shoreline from the restless water beyond, segueing into clusters of mountain peaks cascading into multiple shades of purple. It was an ambitious project.

Many nights the boys would come home from a late night basketball game at the school and find me in the garage, weaving.

They joked, "Pretty soon you will be covered in cobwebs from working out here so long."

I produced five large art pieces before being dragged away to the pressing problems concerning the renovation. One large circular hanging depicted the mountains behind our home, smoky mists and mountain peaks fading into the northern horizon. To portray this I used ten cascading shades of blue, using my own hand spun wool. Another eight foot long ocean scene was an additional piece that also came from the set-up in the garage. It used hemp rope, silver cording, wools and twigs. I loved the twigs.

My girlfriend said, "I knew you'd turn out something special. You are so creative, whether it's with weaving, food or décor for the house."

ORANGE ROLL WITH TEA/GRAND MARNIER

This is a simple cake roll, perfect for an afternoon get together to show off my current weaving creation or my new kitchen. The use of strong tea is an unusual flavoring.

Preheat oven, 325

Cake
Sheet pan, parchment paper
7 eggs, separated
1 cup cake flour, sifted
¼ tsp. baking soda
Pinch salt
1 cup sugar
Juice and zest of 1 medium orange

Method
Beat egg whites adding salt until it begins to form soft peaks.
Add ¼ of the sugar, and beat until stiff, and the mixture is not grainy to your fingers.
Beat yolks, remaining sugar and orange juice until thick.
Add zest. Fold into whites.
Sift flour and soda. Fold into whites/yolks mixture.
Spread onto greased, parchment lined sheet pan.
Bake at 325 for 15 minutes.
Turn out onto a sugared tea towel.
Peel off paper and roll up cake in towel until cool.

¼ cup strong tea
¼ cup grand Marnier
1 cup heavy cream, whipped

Assembly
Unroll cake, ponge, (lightly soak,) surface with tea/liqueur
mixture.
Spread whipped cream over and re-roll cake.
Garnish with powdered sugar and thin orange slices and extra
whipped cream.

11

Four Seasons Leisure World

While I was immersed in weaving, there was a plan brewing that I didn't know anything about. Anton called from his office and said, "Can you meet me for lunch at the Mercury/Lincoln Dealership in North Vancouver?" I tried to find out what was up but he just said, "We'll talk about it when you get there." I hurried to finish my routine at the house, changed my clothes and drove down to North Vancouver ready to have lunch. Why were we meeting at this location? It wasn't a restaurant, but...

Anton was there at the entrance and waved me over to meet two men standing in the showroom of the dealership. They looked important, dressed in expensive suits.

"Meet my new partners." I was baffled, shook hands and waited for an explanation. Partners?

Anton's clients, especially at tax time, took all his energy; it was not unusual to find him working into the night for weeks before the due date when all the paperwork had to be filed. He was five years into this routine when he mentioned one day, in a casual aside, that he had a set of clients who were making huge profits from their Mercury/

Lincoln Dealership. This company also encompassed used cars, sports clothing, and power boats. His whole conversation hadn't registered with me because it was part of Anton's world, not a concern of mine

When going over the numbers with them, Anton had advised them how to handle all their profits and what to invest in. They suggested, "Why don't you spend all your expertise just on our company, be our comptroller?" Anton thought what an inspired idea. This seemed like an offer too good to turn down. They wanted that professional image. He felt sure of their sincerity and was comfortable with them as he had been doing their annual tax work for several years.

Without my knowledge, he put in motion the sale of his accountancy practice, readying him for the move. He thought it was a wonderful plan, using his mathematical brain in a more creative way, just tailor-made for him. No more midnight runs to the post office, dating clients' yearly financials to make the tax deadline. His accountancy practice had yielded a good income, but now this alliance steered us in an exciting new direction.

The four of us went to lunch, toasted each other all around, and on a handshake, we were into new waters. This opportunity opened up endless tangents for material goods. From the used car lots, Anton picked out an almost new 450 SL Mercedes for himself. From the sports store, I shopped through the ski suits, the expensive European models, and said to the store clerk, "Please, just put that on our account." So wonderful!

New ski boots every year for us all. The cars and sports equipment would add up to thousands of dollars if bought retail by someone without Anton's position. Now with the promise of such a lucrative future, this was why he was extravagant with all the details of our house renovation, adding upgrades everywhere. We could afford it. He never asked for my input or considered the possibilities of setbacks.

SIMPLE CRÈME CARAMEL WITH VODKA BERRIES

When we sealed the deal with Four Seasons, we had all the partners and wives to dinner the next night. I served this simple custard/berry dessert as the final note to our new beginning. (I always put up a few jars when the fruit is in season,) and have these preserves available for fruit sauces and desserts.

Bake 325, 30 minutes in a water bath, (see note)
Serves 6-8
Small custard cups

Easy

⅓ cup sugar

6 eggs
2 cups whole milk
1 cup heavy cream
1 Tbsp. vanilla

Method

Put sugar in heavy bottom small pot. Heat sugar without stirring until golden.
Divide syrup among 6-8 small 6oz. custard cups.

Pour mixture through fine mesh sieve into custard cups.
(Note) Use 2" roaster pan deep enough for the ramekins or dish to accommodate hot water to come half-way up dish.
Place cups in this water bath in center of the oven.

Bake 30 minutes or until tops are golden and jiggle slightly.
Do not over bake.
Cool, and chill.
When ready, rinse each plate with cold water. (This helps to position custard on center of plate in case it is a bit off.) Turn out onto plate.
Surround with preserved berries.

Berries
1 qt. berries in season
1 cup vodka
1 cup cognac
1 Tbsp. sugar

Method
Place berries in glass jar and steep for several hours or longer.

12
Sailing

Throughout my marriage I was a strong supporter of the many deals that Anton created. I trusted him. In just one day, on a handshake with a bank manager, we owned The Harrison Hot Springs Spa Resort in the interior of British Columbia: another day, a beautiful, historic, waterfront home on Vancouver Island next to Butchart Gardens. The bank manager funneled all the cool deals to Anton first. They had a tight working arrangement. A gold mine in Pinos, Mexico came from a deal in the stock market; we had thousands of free shares, and it was very speculative. This was an unusual prize. We owned more than just the mine. We owned the whole town, jail and all! As you can tell, I was very amazed with this deal.

I was ensconced in a glamorous hotel on the beach in Mazatlan, Mexico while Anton checked out the mine with the gold in the far-off hills. One hot sunny afternoon in front of my hotel, I splashed in the surf when I was surprised by a suave, dark-haired man swimming toward me speaking in a smooth, Spanish accent.

He said, "Would you like to spend a romantic afternoon with me? I see you are here alone" I was speechless, naïve, shocked. All I could reply was, "Of course not!" and haughtily swam away. Anton returned from the mines and our life continued. No sign of my amour the rest of our stay, thank goodness.

Acquiring a beautiful and expensive sailing sloop from Sweden was Anton's pièce de résistance. I had become good friends with a Swedish family who had just arrived in Vancouver to take up the posting of Swedish Trade Commissioner for Canada.

Lisel and Jorge Larson were young and had children the same age as ours. One night over several glasses of Scotch, Jorge showed us a glamorous brochure picturing a 33 ½ ft. sailing yacht for sale, a brand new sloop, built in Götenborg, Sweden. He talked about his extensive sailing experience in Sweden so it all sounded possible. This sloop could become part of his landed Swedish household goods and be exempt from import taxes should we decide to get in on the deal. Both husbands worked out the finances and made a commitment that night to import this amazing craft to Vancouver.

Our prize arrived at Vancouver's harbor, lashed down to a large wooden cradle on the bow of a freighter. Standing at dockside, I whispered, "Could that really belong to us?"

Years of sailing adventures beckoned us all. Six enthusiastic boys, our three and the Larson's three all started sailing lessons at the nearby Ambleside Sailing Club in West Vancouver. Anton did not know how to sail, but understood tides, how to tie up/anchor-off in the tricky waters of the Puget Sound from his summers aboard his father's salmon Seine boat, the "Beachy Head." The sailing part came easily to him. He was confident as usual! I didn't know how to sail so I joined the ladies sailing group in West Van. We all learned quickly and soon felt experienced and safe. Sand in our shoes became second nature. After the first year, we bought out our partner for $10,000 and had the boat to ourselves.

Remembering those precious ten years when we were so together as a family was priceless. Sailing, laughing at twenty knot gusting winds, our adrenalin was high. The boys groaned when the wind died, knowing the Volvo engine would be turned on: the indication for the kids to furl the sails. There would be a moment of quiet before we were under way with the drumming of the engine. The fishing lines came out on deck and the thrill of power by blustery wind and waves was gone until the next blow.

David was first to go below, "I'm going to put on some music," he said, not so interested in fishing. Anthony started for the foredeck saying, "It's time for relaxing." Paul waited patiently, hands on the wheel, reading the waves, steady on the compass, steering for our next port, ready to bring everyone to life again when white caps started to curl. Anton was the only avid fisherman.

Before long Paul shouted out orders, "Wind's up, Anthony! Set the jib, watch you head, boom swinging over. Look lively, now!" Everyone scrambled and we on our way again, with the sails billowing out like soft marsh-mellows. We were under the power of the sea and wind. The empty fishing lines were stowed away, Anton killed the engine.

Later in the day we saw a small commercial trawler in a deserted bay. It was anchored-off for the night. We also secured our sloop, making sure the anchor was dug into the sand and rocks deep below.

Possibly the trawler would have fresh iced shrimp or crab for our dinner that evening. The boys rowed over in our dinghy and called out to the mate on deck, "Do you have fish or seafood for sale?" They excitedly rowed back and brought a big, plastic bag of whole crab for all of us to devour. So fresh, so delicious, so amazing! After dinner and all the clean-up, the boys were finally bunked down, worn out and called it a day.

Anton and I went up top at midnight, stretched out naked on the deck, the teak still warm against our skin. We gazed up to wonder about the vast, darkened universe showering us with falling stars that streaked across our velvet cocoon.

I daydreamed, could our life be this perfect? I felt so lucky to have such wonderful boys and the perfect husband. Was it too good to be true? We were sharing a closeness that I realized had been missing for some time; we talked about the boys, their accomplishments, how well they were doing, university, their future and our own destiny.

Looking into his eyes I said, "Are you okay. Are you really happy? Are you?" He was thoughtful for a moment, then kissed me hard and said,

"Yes, first the 'practice' and now Four Seasons has paid off very well. We've acquired some good stuff: it's good for us as a family. I love my life, I love you." When he said stuff, he meant material things. We stayed there for some time, entwined, making passionate love with only the stars above to see us, the water below a silky stillness. Finally we went down to the aft cabin to continue to dream.

We were heading for Maple Bay, near Victoria, on the tip of Vancouver Island, to enter an annual summer regatta for all size boats. Our sailing friends, Terry and Chickie Buckholtz from Seattle would be there too. We looked forward to a boisterous reunion, sailing talk and catching up on all their news.

Their girls, teenaged Julie and Janet, were good sailors. The bay was crowded with all kinds of yachts and boats. Everyone hoped for bragging rights as the two days of races began.

Terry owned an Audi/BMW/Rolls Royce dealership in Seattle. Of course the guys talked cars and business, and Chickie and I jabbered on about food, the kids and their activities.

BARBARA'S PIZZA

Crusts can be frozen plain or filled. I would take these pizzas on board for our first night out on the sailboat. When we had sailed or motored about 2 hours, they were ready to pop into a hot galley oven. Until I had my sea legs, less time in the cabin was preferred.

Oven 400
Bake 20 minutes

Easy

Basic dough-2 crusts
1 tsp. sugar
½ cup lukewarm water
1 package= (1 tb. yeast)
2 Tbsp. vegetable oil
2½ -3 cups all-purpose flour, can be unbleached or variations
I tsp salt
½ cup water

Method
Dissolve sugar in lukewarm water, then sprinkle yeast over water. Allow to stand 10 minutes to proof.
Blend in oil.
Mix ½ cup flour with salt and adding ½ cup additional water with the above yeast mixture. Blend to create starter dough.
Knead in remaining flour a little at a time to medium, non-sticky dough.

Brush with oil, put in a warm pottery bowl, covering with plastic to let rise in a warm place, (lowest setting in a pre-warmed oven, turned off) is a good spot. Allow to double in bulk.

Punch dough down, divide in two or more depending on pizza size.

Lightly grease pan.

Stretch dough to fit pans, add toppings and let sit 20 minutes. Bake in 400 oven about 20 minutes.

Toppings

Olive oil, tomato sauce, oregano, mozzarella, shredded cheddar, sliced olives, pepperoni, bell peppers, mushrooms, pineapple tidbits, smoky ham.

SWEDISH GRAVLAX

Here is the basic recipe that our friends from Sweden shared with me. Gravlax is very expensive to buy in a specialty store but see how easy it is to make. Use this for any party menu, especially for Christmas or the beginning of the Swedish summer holiday, the festival of lights.

Easy

Gravlax

Whole boned out salmon **filet**, skin on, size determined by requirements.

For a 10 lb. salmon, the ratio of ingredients is as follows.
2 bunches of fresh dill
1 bottle of vodka, brandy, aquavit or similar liquor.
2 lb. coarse, Kosher salt
2 lb. granulated sugar
2 cups of fresh cracked black pepper

Method

In a large glass or stainless roaster or pan large enough to lay salmon, flat and deep enough to accommodate ingredients, layer salmon under and over with above ingredients.
Cover with plastic wrap, weight down and refrigerate
48 hours.
Turn piece over several times to marinate all surfaces.
During curing, liquid will form from fish and fish will become firm.
Rinse off slightly, leaving some of the peppercorns and dill etc.

Slice very thin on the bias as for smoked salmon.
Serve with Russian black bread or cocktail rounds, horseradish mustard and dill sauce.

Sauce

1 cup Dijon mustard
2 Tbsp. dry mustard
½ cup sugar
⅓ cup white wine vinegar
1 bunch fresh dill, minced
1½ cups peanut oil

Method

Place all ingredients except oil in processor. Blend. Now slowly add oil, blending, just like making mayonnaise. Chill. Serve with cured Gravlax, or smoked salmon.

13

Olympics

Back home, Paul still in middle school, represented Vancouver in dozens of sailing regattas. Over two years, he was kept busy with yachting events in Vancouver, Seattle, Montreal, San Francisco, Brazil and Hawaii.

In 1972 he was chosen to represent Canada at the Junior Sailing Olympics in Travemünde, Germany. We sent him off at fifteen to travel across the world with his one crew and a rudder. At the airport, we hugged, held our breath and off he went with all our prayers. He didn't win. Just to go was fabulous for the experience that would enrich his life with exposure to different cultures and languages.

We arranged tickets for both boys to get to Yugoslavia after the races in Germany finished. They would visit Anton's relatives living in a small village below Split on the Croatian coastline. We did worry about the boys. Of course! We heard later that they had been let off from a commuter bus on a dusty road somewhere near Tuçepi, on the Adriatic. Late in the day, as they trudged along with their duffle bags and heavy rudder, a car approached. They waved it down for some directions and because they didn't speak the language, Paul said in

English, "Miachika, Tuçepi," pointing to himself. The driver waved excitedly, he said in broken English, "Me cousin, we expect you," and hugged them, stowed their gear, motioned them to jump in and away they went, right to the home of the Miachika clan. What a lucky ending.

It had been forty five years since Anton, a boy of seven with his mother, left their homeland on a freighter bound for a new life in Canada. Paul was the first of our family to return to Anton's birthplace.

One lasting thing the boys learned from our years of sailing; be cautious and be prepared for the dangerous power of the sea and wind. Anton's own father had died, swept overboard several years ago in a commercial boating disaster on the "Beachy Head" while returning down the stormy west coast of British Columbia from Alaska.

14

Custom Cheesecakes

The Four Seasons Leisure World partnership lasted only three years. Suddenly Anton was out, no longer a partner. As crazy as this appears, he didn't have a written agreement with the other two partners, so he had nothing to fall back on! It sounded so wrong, a professional business man as he was, to have endangered our existence with such a casual move. He had just gone on their word, a handshake. Really stupid on his part, but I held my tongue. He had sold his accounting practice to an associate before joining Four Seasons, so now he really needed to look forward, and had to create something new.

Months passed and our lives drifted along in much the same affluent fashion. We still belonged to all the country clubs; we still owned two Mercedes, the blue 450 SL and a handsome 1962 silver, 300 SL roadster, a silver Jaguar and a station wagon. We appeared to be happy to the outside world. Such a façade!

In the midnight hours I was terrified. Worry had gotten me nowhere and I wasn't sleeping. I didn't want to believe my life was in jeopardy, that my life was starting to unravel. I kept reliving the day he had come home so wild and out of control. I would never know why he had lost his position at Four Seasons. About finances, he just refused to tell, would not discuss the bank or money! I needed to be honest with myself and face the worst. He wasn't working. I needed a plan for my future, but it all seemed so vague. I couldn't bring myself to tell anyone. I kept thinking he would work it out, as he always came up roses before. I know families have problems but they eventually get straightened out. Anton's mother wasn't any help, she glossed over his excessive drinking, refusing to see the dangers.

At night in an alcoholic stupor, pacing up and down the hallway, he screamed at me, "You don't understand anything, you are just a stupid housewife, plus more demeaning words with F... and C...," I can't bring myself to write but it cut me deeply, however, I still stayed and trusted him. Years ago I had pledged, "For Better or Worse."

He drifted through several more years, yes years, drinking, dis-illusioned and disappointed with himself. Four Seasons had left him defeated. He couldn't face starting over at something, and wouldn't adjust. The future was a big, black obstacle to him. I knew he had to be cashing out our investments to stay afloat. Selling stocks some months created instant money; then selling our sailboat brought in sixty thousand cash, our beautiful sail boat was gone. Somehow I still trusted him. My subconscious pushed all the bad stuff down. This was not how my life was supposed to go.

My existence had to change. Anton's financial meltdown during the first part of my life is what pushed me forward. It sounds easy to accept this conclusion, but let me regress into my deepest thoughts. I finally accepted that my husband was no longer my safe haven. It had taken me many months, then years to face the awful truth. I was now desperately trying to think of what I could do to make a living.

I had been a homemaker, never part of the business world for over thirty years; but I did have my baking skills. My delicious cheesecakes were currently the subject of interest at a prominent restaurant in West Van. The manager had ordered several cakes as a test a few weeks before and was ecstatic over the quality and delicate flavor. He encouraged me to commit four cakes a week for their clientele. He said "This will make our restaurant different. We can't afford a pastry chef on site, but your desserts will give us something homemade and special." I delivered my cheesecakes in the big trunk of our silver Jaguar. I now had 8 spring form pans. Maybe this was the start of a new direction for me. But I still viewed it as a hobby. I never dreamed this lark, this hobby, free- lanced pastries to friends and acquaintances would be my meal ticket to post marriage, widow security.

BARBARA'S NEW YORK CHEESECAKE

In the 60's Cheesecake was a new dessert that was considered very chic. Everyone loved it and many variations exist now but this was the original. Later I won a national contest with "Mascarpone Cheesecake," using only half of the plain cream cheese plus one container, 8oz. of Mascarpone Italian cream cheese. Anyway, start with this one, maybe branch out.

Oven 350
Serves 12
9'spring form pan

Easy

Crust
12 double graham crackers, crushed
2 Tbsp. sugar
⅓ cup melted butter

2- 8 oz. packages plain cream cheese (1-lb.)
½ cup sugar
4 eggs
1 tsp vanilla
1 tsp lemon juice and zest

Topping
4 oz. sour cream
1 tsp vanilla
3 tsp sugar

Method

Preheat oven 350. Place rack in lower ⅓ of oven.

Grease bottom and sides of pan.

Melt butter and add to cracker crumbs and sugar.

Mix well and press onto bottom and up sides of greased pan.

Beat cream cheeses on medium, add sugar; add eggs one at a time blending well. See note.

Add vanilla, lemon juice and zest.

Pour into ready pan.

Bake at 350 for 25 minutes. (Do not over bake).

Beat sour cream, sugar and flavouring.

Pour over top of cake, spreading evenly to outside edges.

Return to oven and bake an additional 10 minutes.

Cool on counter, then refrigerate in pan, 4 hours or over-night.

Release from cake pan, serve plain or with fruit sauce blueberry or raspberry.

Note, when adding eggs, mix slowly to blend all but not adding extra air for a finished smooth, creamy filling.

15

Cuisine de Barbara

With the looming threat of no income at age forty-four, future vacations and travel that we had planned and worked so hard to afford in these middle years, were put on hold. The bedroom wing was still unfinished. He now had his precious full-sized pool table in the expanded family room. My heart's desire kitchen with its huge gas guzzling stove seemed like a frivolous present. Maybe the butcher block counters, custom marble pastry slab, glass cabinets and gleaming stainless equipment were too extravagant. Anton had not projected the costs accurately. With his prestigious position at Four Seasons suddenly gone, where would the money come from now? It had all snowballed. This last renovation was too ambitious, but I did have a perfect work area.

I said, "It will be my new base of operations." I still wanted to travel and a cooking school might make it happen. I had no real concept of our true finances, but everything still seemed possible. Anton refused to discuss our money, so I still didn't understand the looming danger of the bank and all that it entailed.

I only knew my parties were always fun and I cooked better than most of our friends. Now I had this wonderful workspace; "I could teach all my best recipes first and possibly make money doing it." Cooking schools in Canada in 1974 were quite a new trend but Cordon Bleu in France had been established for years, so maybe it wasn't so crazy. If I started a cooking school, then I could travel to France, Italy and Yugoslavia adding important diplomas and confidence to my presentations. Refocusing my thoughts, this crazy idea floated into my mind. Right at that second, sitting on the floor, a zany inspiration appeared. I said out loud to my kitchen walls, "I'm going to start my own cooking school." The fact that I had no real culinary credentials didn't occur to me at first. I was a passionate cook, it felt right. I had to act, to take the chance. At last I was jolted into action, thought I might save us. I was the one to step forward and make the choices.

My cooking school idea was a good one. No time to reminisce. I forced myself to sit down and think it through, plan something ahead.

Perhaps Zorka, Anton's sister, younger by seven years, could be a sort of partner. She was a good cook and fine homemaker but lacked certain flair. I knew I needed someone to be a helper. We had always been on friendly terms, just part of the family. Would she think it was a put-down to be a side-kick, or would she be excited to be part of my exciting new adventure? Maybe she would expect to be an equal partner. We got together to hash out some ideas.

Zorka said, "What do you see, what sort of recipes should we include, and where would it all take place?" She didn't offer much. "What about a name?" Lots of questions but no answers. It was left up to me.

I said, "Of course the school would be in my spacious remodeled kitchen with my huge, new, Wolf stove." As we talked, themes, recipes and my proposal to work together were laid out. Any profits should be 50-50. I wanted to be fair. Several think-tank sessions later, more details emerged.

Everyone knew me by "Babs," my nickname from high school and college, but Cuisine de Babs didn't sound quite right so I went back to my given name and called my venture Cuisine de Barbara. Now I hatched a style for the first set of classes. The first series of six classes would be sort of French cooking. French was the stepping off point for most recipes, using lots of technique with classic dishes woven into each lesson.

Zorka's job was to type my recipes. My job was to think up a marketing strategy, and set out a professional looking brochure that described our new school. I placed an advertisement in the local paper and nervously wondered, "Will anyone come?" Vancouver noticed my little announcement and the phone started to ring.

I planned to offer a complete image; recipes, preparation techniques, shopping sources, table settings, timing, tips about each recipe, presentation, décor, wine- appreciation and floral design. At first I could teach all my most reliable ideas, the tried and true. It would be great having students in my kitchen.

Very grandiosely I named my first classes, "The French Series." I wasn't French, nor could I really speak French but I thought French. The first six menus came to mind quickly with recipes I thought everyone would like to cook. I carefully chose items that were precise and had interesting preparation techniques, or were a bit tricky. Dishes that needed boning, or skinning and dishes prepared with pastry. "Look, this is how to hold your knife to cut up chicken. This is how to handle and fillet a whole salmon and pull out the pin bones. Whisk egg whites like this to a perfect no-fail peak, not too dry but just right. See how simple baked soufflés are, not mysterious at all."

The first series covered savory crepes, soups, filet of beef, salmon, veal, meringues and tortes. Classes often included more than one dessert. I said, "My favourite part of the meal is dessert and two are better than one."

My opening menu for The French Series, six lessons was

Potage de la Dureau
Piquant Duckling
Baby Vegetables
Wild Rice
Tomato Saucers
Hot Lemon Soufflés
Chocolate Almond Torta

Everything had to be planned for timing and smooth preparation. When you hold yourself up there as an expert, it better be good! With three ovens I was able to have several items going on at the same time. While doing prep-technique I asked, "Who knows how to cut onions like this?" Or, "I hope straining this soup in a food mill isn't too boring but it's important. It gives a great texture! Does everyone own a food mill? Many people have no idea what to do with poultry let alone a duck!" We talked about knives and I demonstrated which one to use for boning.

Some students said, "I could never do that." But I just told them,

"Be confident." I proceeded to show how to dissect it into pieces and that made a good effect. After roasting the duck parts in a hot oven, the finished result was pink and juicy inside with the skin crispy. Everyone applauded. I was having a good time.

HOT LEMON SOUFFLÉS

Lemon soufflés are a chic finish for any dinner. It was a chance to use my petite porcelain molds and show how to whisk and create a soufflé.
This fabulous dessert came from lesson One, The French Series.
Medium difficulty, but read the recipe all through and you will see it is very straight forward.

4- 6, ¾ cup small ramekins
Oven 425

Medium

Serves 4-6

Soufflé base
½ cup granulated sugar, divided
Also extra sugar to coat ramekins
4 Tbsp. unsalted butter
⅓ cup fresh lemon juice
4 large egg <u>yolks</u>
1 Tbsp. finely grated lemon zest
5 large egg whites, room temperature
Confectioners' sugar for dusting plate

Method
In a medium non-reactive sauce pot, combine ¼ cup of the granulated sugar, the butter and the lemon juice and cook over moderate heat, stirring until sugar and butter are melted.

Remove from heat, stir in egg yolks one at a time, mixing well after each addition.
Add lemon zest, back over moderate heat, stirring until thickened, coating the back of a silver spoon.
Be careful, not to boil or it will curdle or scrambled the eggs.
This can be prepared up to this point. Cover, refrigerate until needed.

Bring to room temperature when ready to finish.
Preheat oven 425

Butter ramekins, dust with sugar. Freeze for ten minutes.
In a medium bowl, free of any grease, beat egg whites on medium until soft peaks. Add remaining sugar and continue beating until whites are glossy and firm, about 2 minutes.
Stir in ¼ of lemon curd to temper the whites mixture, then fold in remainder of curd.

Fill molds to top.
Smooth each one with cake spatula; run thumb around inner rim to make a cap to form while baking.

Bake in lower ⅓ of oven for about 13 minutes for ramekins or more for large baker.
When nicely browned and puffed, firm on edges, remove from oven, dust with confectioners' sugar and serve at once.

16

'Just Desserts,' a New Series

I was engrossed in marketing my classes, creating original recipes and complete menus into more complicated programs to entice existing students to return to each new series as I thought them up. It still felt like a hobby, but I was serious in my efforts.

Paperwork, testing recipes for timing, and selling the classes person to person or over the phone was hard work but I filled my kitchen. To stay ahead, I was constantly researching new trends.

As the courses multiplied, I kept a master sheet on each class making notes and comments to myself, perfecting my performance. I realized the students were equally important as the food. As a teacher I needed to ensure they absorbed my passion as each new recipe was completed.

I reveled in the idea of a dessert course. Pulling together some of my trusted showstoppers I launched 'Just Desserts', a six-lesson series.

Coeur à la Crème was one of the easy ones. Creamy, easy to make but just a bit out of the ordinary when using darling little heart shaped ramekins, it is a perfect finish for any dinner or luncheon. Orange Bavarian torte was another.

COEUR À LA CRÈME

This is a creamy dessert, so easy to make and is always delicious. Culled from a set of classes in a series I called Just Desserts. Be sure to notice that you need to have cheesecloth on hand, and molds with small holes for drainage. Use this dessert for Valentine's Day and get rave revues. This is my go-to dessert for many occasions. ." (Don't confuse this custard with all the other ones. This one isn't baked. The others are Crème Caramel, with the caramel on the bottom like a flan, while Crème Brûlée has the crunchy caramel on the top, and Nouvelle Crème Brûlée has the crusted baguette on top and then grilled.
Anyway here is Coeur a la Crème.

No baking
4-6 oz. porcelain heart or ramekin molds or one large heart mold.
Easy

½ lb. of cottage cheese
1 cup heavy cream
¼ cup plain cream cheese
3 Tbsp. powdered sugar
½ tsp vanilla

Fresh or frozen raspberries,
1 tsp. orange flavored honey
1 Tbsp. Kirsch

Cheesecloth
Small heart ceramic molds or one large one

Method

Dip squares of cheesecloth in water with a splash of lemon juice.

Position cloth over molds with enough hanging over the sides to allow for over-wrapping.

Rub cottage cheese through a fine sieve. Set aside.

Beat cream cheese to smooth consistency. Set aside.

Whip cream to medium stiff peaks.

In medium bowl, fold cheese, cream cheese and whipped cream together, add flavouring.

Fill molds, smooth tops, fold cloth over. Set molds on rack and sheet pan to rest overnight, allowing any moisture to drop from bottom of molds.

Puree berries, adding honey and flavouring, creating what is called a Coulis, an uncooked berry sauce.

Fold back cloth, un-mold desserts onto dessert plates, surround with sauce, add mint leaf or sprinkle minced leaves for plate decoration, (optional).

17

An Extra Hand

The first six months flew by and I was pouring myself into each presentation. At the end of a class when the room cleared, I said, "Wow, what a rush!" The students were absorbing it all. I was thrilled to explain the footprint, history, and theory as I worked.

When I had a few days between classes, the truth needed to be addressed. Zorka was not a perfect choice for a partner: to divide any profits 50-50 was not sitting well in my gut now. The work load was skewed. I was doing almost everything; the planning, the testing, the shopping. We needed to clear the air no matter how painful the results. I was lying awake at night anxious about the family fall-out. How would I tell Zorka the school idea wasn't working between us? Right away I had a moral dilemma. As soon as we sat down Zorka said,

"I know this is not working between us. I can't be here as much as is necessary to carry my side, to be really helpful." So that was it.

I thought we parted ways on a friendly note but was this just a façade on her part? At first, my daughter-in-law Victoria stepped in, adding her language expertise with French and Italian words, but as a newlywed it was more than she wanted or had time to do. She and Anthony had their own household to set up. Then an energetic student stepped in to be my helper. A trade off: cooking experience for her at no cost, a helper for me for free.

Joanne said, "Let me be your extra hand." It was the perfect solution.

18
I.A.C.P. Meeting Julia

My school was gaining momentum like a run-away train. In the April issue of a current food magazine, I noticed an advert for a conference under the auspices of a new group called "International Association of Cooking Schools, I.A.C.S. later to be called I.AC.P, Cooking Professionals. This meeting was to be in San Francisco the following March, almost a year away.

I said to Anton, "This would be a great opportunity to be in on the latest contacts and food trends. It is expensive to go there and pay hotel and conference costs but I'm sure it will be worth it."

Anton said, "I think it's a good marketing idea. Find out some more about the founding members and how to register." I planned to go on my own. I wanted to dabble my fingers into this new world and needed to be in charge.

They offered an option to share a room. It might be fun and less expensive. The months rolled by and before long I was getting ready to think about what this conference might bring.

San Francisco had so much to offer. The event was at the St. Francis Hotel, one of the old grand hotels of the city. After checking in, I rolled my luggage over to the elevators and saw a lady there with the same group lapel tag, so I excitedly introduced myself. Sharon Tyler Herbst was friendly and eager to invite me into this inner group of food enthusiasts.

She said, "I am pleased to meet you, you're from Vancouver, I see. I'm from LA. I'm sure we will cross paths." With that we both stepped in to the waiting elevator and were whisked up to our floor. As she stepped out, Sharon said, "See you at the registration table for the conference." I was making friends already.

This was the beginning of many wonderful conferences to come. By the next year, my new friend had authored a book '*All about Bread*.' When she signed my copy it read, "Hi Barbara, you were the first lady I met at last year's conference, Happy Baking." Many years later Sharon published an intensive resource for all baking and cooking called, *The Food Lover's Companion*.

The I.A.C.P. had many famous members right from the start. At that first conference, I met Julia Child and had my picture taken with her. She was the guest speaker and an honored member. Her humorous mannerisms and odd speaking voice was really her style. At this same conference, I became aware of Jacques Pépin, the famous French chef and author of several important food/teaching books. I was ready and eager to be swept into this world.

I tried to attend all the future conferences when possible. When working for Guckenheimer, from 1986-1989, the company paid the fee, and I was able to bring back important new trends for them. Even by 1997 when I was self-employed and had to support all my own expenses, I kept in touch with all the schools and food importers: my trail to the culinary stars and wholesale products. It was an important group, these 'foodies'!

Julia Child and Barbara at the I.A.C.P. San Francisco Conference

19

Cooking lesson with Jacques

In a glossy, American food magazine, I noticed a class offered in July, 1976, in San Mateo, California. It featured international chef Jacques Pepin. I left the article out for Anton to see, and I suggested we could take a mini vacation to San Francisco; I could join the class, and seek out unusual restaurants and destinations in San Francisco like Bix, Aqua and Yang Sing. We could travel to the wine country to find the French Laundry in Napa Valley. We could write it off because I had this idea …

I had this idea of promoting a ten day trip to San Francisco and Napa Valley, taking my students on a custom experience for food, fun and travel. I could work with the airlines for best group fare, research other costs when doing the initial trip with Anton, and build a really great adventure. I was sure my students would love it, they trusted me.

Anton agreed to go. Once away from home, he was a wonderful traveler. We held hands, joked, drank martinis, made love in the soft downy sheets of the big bed at the luxurious St. Francis Hotel, a famous landmark in the center of San Francisco. The next morning we ordered breakfast in our room and felt like rock stars.

The class Jacques gave was fabulous; I was so impressed. There were twelve participants, but I made sure I introduced myself, saying, "Your class was so awesome." We exchanged cards. It was a start. I could impress everyone in my next class. I had learned how to make butter roses, just a small thing but a special touch to the dinner table. I loved the techniques. Jacques continued to surprise us all with so many other *trucs* from his vast depth of experience and knowledge as he worked through his menus.

Here is the perfect finished butter rose

JACQUES PÉPIN'S LIVER PÂTÉ AND BUTTER ROSES LESSON

Jacques is the perfect chef, never wasting any part of a food item. He demonstrated a delightful pâté using <u>equal</u> parts livers, (calves, chicken or beef) butter and caramelized onions.

Mix ingredients together in a processor. Strain all through a fine sieve to remove any gristly bits.

Pile into a decorative dish and top off with a tomato rose or one of his carved butter roses. Dust with minced parsley. Follow the above for this tasty and inexpensive pâté, so easy I'm not even writing up a real recipe, just follow the ratios above.

Butter Roses, Décoration en Beurre

To make a butter rose or flower, use a chilled bar or block of butter to start.

Have beside you a cup of chilled ice water. as you scrape each piece of butter with a paring knife, drop the butter strip into the ice water.

Next pick it up with your fingers and wrap it into a bud. Drop back in the cold water.

With the same knife, pull more strips and wind around the first piece.

Continue to create an open flower.

Keep flower in the ice water and finally with the tip of your knife, set it on a fresh block of butter. Keep chilled until needed. Add a piece of parsley or other garnish.

20

St. Helena, Napa

Our excursion to Napa Valley began with a stop at the Oakville Grocery, a local food haunt supplying the best baguettes, pâtés, condiments, pastries and of course wine. We found a grassy park, spread out a blanket and enjoyed our gourmet picnic.

It was soon time to check into the St. Helena Hotel, a quaint structure on Main Street in the middle of this little historic town. This could be a good place for my student's home base and surprisingly it was not too expensive. While in town, I called a contact to arrange special introductions to wineries and restaurants. The bakery shops were alluring, showing baguettes, artisan breads, tarts and chocolates with aromas floating out the screened front doors. A big basket of wispy, thin, chocolate wafers in one of the display windows caught my eye. Everything in the bakery was mouth-watering, delicious.

Our first evening, we dined at the Auberge du Soleil, highly recommended by food writers and locals. The restaurant and spa was high on Rutherford Hill, looking back over the valley, near the Silverado Trail, We arrived a bit early so we could enjoy the sunset.

The Maître d' promptly seated us at a favorable center table near a window. Amazing, what a view! Anton passed the wine list over to me saying, "You're the expert." By chance, I chose Flora Springs Chardonnay. The waiter presented the bottle for my approval, he opened it and poured a tidbit in mine to taste. I took a small sip, closed my eyes to heighten the experience, tasting mellow pears and crisp apple undertones, opened my eyes and said, "Yumm," meaning a definite yes: then he poured Anton's goblet, smiled with a little nod to a nearby table, and handed me a business card. He said, "This is from that table over there, they want you to have this wine complimentary."

Wow, we were so surprised and pleased. The back of the card had a note. It said, "If you have time, please visit us at our winery tomorrow," signed Flora. We waved, smiled, enjoyed the superb bottle and had a great dinner. When our neighbors finished their dinner, they explained, "We are still so excited when we hear someone ordering our wine." We thanked them profusely and made plans to visit the next day.

Floras's family was so inviting, we felt really special. Their main structure was a large, stone building, impressive, the property inherited from the Martini family some years back. The Flora boys attended well known Davis University in Sacramento for a highly valuable degree in viticulture and wine production. We saw first-hand what made their wine so special. Years later I met Flora Sr. over lunch at the Century Club in San Francisco, where I was the Executive Chef. She remembered me and we had a nice chat.

The rest of our stay in the valley provided more wine, wonderful food and great shopping at many small boutiques. This trip was charmed.

Back home, I could hardly wait to pull together all the details for my "Tour." I culled through the chits for all our expenses, got busy on the calculator, and devised a cost effective plan. I needed a flyer with an all-inclusive price to advertise my trip. This would be sold as a girls' getaway. No need to worry about tipping, costs, taxis, or restaurant arrangements. I would cover it all! I was sure my students would love it.

I said to them, "Just get to the airport and all else is on me." This was my hook, my way to sell it. It's the carefree way I wanted to travel. In no time I had twelve excited participants signed up and ready to go. It would be all a great success.

At home, Anton got up late, dressed in one of his perfect suits and casually said, "I'll be at the club to meet some friends on business, don't wait dinner for me." I had hopes, but what he really meant was, "I'm meeting my buddies for drinks and BS."

When we returned from my culinary tour, nothing had changed for him. He had pulled back in his shell, he was still adrift.

I thought, "Our life will get on track soon. If I keep working hard he will be challenged to find a new direction too." I had already nagged enough, now he had to act.

LARGE CHOCOLATE TUILES, (COOKIES)

These chocolate wafers were in a bakery window on Main Street in St. Helena. I researched my own recipe collection and here it is. The Tuiles are so crispy. They pair wonderfully with a flute of Mocha Mousse or Vanilla ice cream to finish off the presentation.

About 60 cookies
Oven 325
Easy

Greased, floured sheet pan or Silipat sheet.

1 cup brown sugar
1 cup granulated sugar
12 egg whites
½ cup flour, maybe a bit more if needed
¼ cup baking cocoa
Pinch cinnamon
½ cup heavy cream
1 cup unsalted butter, melted
1 tsp. water
Sliced almonds, toasted

Method
Preheat oven.
Prepare sheet pans.
Whisk sugars and egg whites in large bowl.
Sift flour, cocoa, salt and cinnamon together, then add to bowl. Add melted butter.

Let sit 5 minutes.
Add water.
Spoon and spread about 2 Tbsp. of the mixture for each
cookie, well apart on sheet. Toss a few sliced almonds on top.

Test texture with one or two to begin. If a bit too thin, add a
touch more flour.
Bake about 8 minutes until surface is dry, loses its shine.
Cool on rack, or shape over glass.
Store the cookies in an air tight tin.

21
Europe Travels

"Anton, look at this itinerary that Harold has helped me put together. I think you should consider returning to Yugoslavia to reacquaint yourself with all your relatives in Tuçepi. It could be a great experience for you. You'd be able to use your Slav language. Besides, there's a cooking class in Venice at a famous hotel, the Gritti Palace, that I could fit in on the way. Look at this plan! We could write some of it off against the cooking school."

In conversations like this with my husband I continued to hint at my hopes for future travel. I was appealing to his business senses. I was suggesting an ambitious six- week trip. "Start on the Amalfi coastline, up to Rome, over to the Eastern Italian coastline, into Venice, then on to Rjieka, Split and Tuçepi in Yugoslavia."

I had started browsing bookstores for first-hand travel guides of Italy and beyond. An excellent sounding travelogue, a book, described small, intimate stops along the coastline, also in Rome and Venice.

I said, "These are the pensions that we are looking for still, undis-covered, inexpensive, uncovered by this enthusiastic writer, it won't cost too much and would be fun. Even the addresses and phone numbers are here." I was optimistic.

Harold, our next door neighbor, owned Holiday Travel. He was old style, English, a very wise, seasoned traveler, and had great advice for our first trip to Europe. He believed that first class was the only way to travel for us, at least to start! "First go to a fabulous palace I know about in Ravello, relax for several days on the Amalfi coastline, and start your trip from there." Anton thought it was a great idea. It was time to regain his roots.

We would fly nonstop from Vancouver to Naples. Harold said, "Rent a car at the airport, immediately drive away, then take the inland route to Ravello." He indicated Naples is a rough city, one to be away from as quickly as possible as there is lots of crime there, (a hint to drive away.) So we followed his suggestion.

I didn't know what to expect. Would everything be so built up, towns crowded together after so many centuries of civilization?

To my delight, it was better than anything I had ever imagined.

Anton said, "Isn't this fabulous, it's so beautiful and so old." As we drove through rolling hills covered in grape vines, big towns, small quaint villages, town squares, and incredible villas, he continued to be as impressed as I was. "Over there, look at that amazing castle, just like a post card." At last, driving south along a dusty, narrow road, we came upon the mystical, hilltop town of Ravello; a place of tiny twisting alleys, winding up through the mists of the azure Mediterranean below.

Our car barely fit through the narrow stone-arched entry at the front of the palace. The owner stepped out to greet us. "Buon giorno" He was exactly what I had imagined; suave, thin, elegant, dressed in an expensive cashmere sweater, Gucci loafers and no socks. This time he said a more informal "hello, welcome." Our host Marco Vuilleumier welcomed us warmly, stepping forward to shake hands as we got out of our small, economy car. Dreamy Palumbo

Palace, boasted such past guests as Humphrey Bogart and Ernest Hemmingway, their autographs preserved in the old, golden Hotel Palumbo register.

The 12 century palace was overwhelming, we were immediately intoxicated with the whole scene. A porter showed us to our room or should I say suite, explained the routine of the palace, breakfast was included of course. He retreated, saying, "Ciao," while closing the heavy oak door, leaving us to discover our new/old surroundings.

Exotic travel magazines could not do this place justice; gauzy drapes fluttered over French doors, opening onto a balustrade that looked down on tile roofs, hillside vines, grazing sheep and the mists off the Mediterranean sea far below. We stepped outside, breathing in the scents of lemon and orange from the steep orchards in the palace gardens. Anton gathered me into his arms and said, "This is the best thing you ever talked me into. I love it. Thank you, thank you!"

Back in the marble lobby, Marco chatted with us in perfect English and before long talk turned to wine.

He said, "Please come with me to the wine cellar beneath the castle." Along musty stone passageways, we saw hundreds of resting bottles. Casually he plucked two dusty bottles of Merlot with the Palumbo label from the racks and gave them to us as a welcoming gift.

Of course he knew every inch of such a small town, so when we asked where to eat he said without doubt, "Mama Rosa's down the road."

Back at the palace, our first bottle of wine emptied as if by magic, as we relaxed in our room, rumpled the sheets, and then lay talking. About nine o'clock hunger set in so we dressed, and walked along to a small taverna called Rosa's. It was busy inside. Where had all these patrons come from? The *maître d'* showed us to the last open table and our gourmet holiday began.

We ordered martinis to start. Lifting our drinks in a toast we waited for our Primi, Secondi and Dolci choices from the menu. Ante-pasta was the first course of rolled Prociutto, local olives, whole, crispy sardines and crusty bread. The second course, Veal Piccata, in a delicate caper sauce, feather light Gnocchi, and touch of baby vegetables from the nearby gardens plus a chilled bottle of rose. The Dolci, dessert course, was superb! Zuccotto also called a Bombé; a dome-shaped layered cake filled with custard cream, nuts and finished with a draped chocolate glaze, a culinary treat I had not tasted before. "This will be perfect for my classes back home." I furtively made notes and sketches of the meal we had just eaten.

ZUCCOTO, A CHOCOLATE COVERED BOMBÉ

Our trip to Yugoslavia began with Ravello. It was high on a mountain side overlooking the blue Mediterranean. Our dinner destination the first night was along a tiny road not far from the palace.. Dessert did not disappoint, it was memorable. This was the start of sketches and ingredients in my handy notepad, used to interpret every nuance when returning home. This would be for my new Italian Series.

Serves 8
A 6 cup stainless round bowl
Easy

2 oz. ground almonds
2 oz. ground hazelnuts
Pound cake, baked or purchased
3 Tbsp. Brandy
3 Tbsp. Kirsch
3 Tbsp. Cointreau
5 oz. semi-sweet chocolate
2 cups whipping cream
1 Tbsp. confectioner's sugar
Glace cherries
8 oz. dark semi-sweet chocolate for glazing

Method

Line a six cup stainless bowl of deep shape, with plastic wrap, allowing overhang.

Cut pound cake into triangle points with the pieces fitting together into bowl
Sprinkle cake with liqueurs.
Whip cream, dividing into 2 bowls, ⅓, ⅔.
Fold 1 oz. melted chocolate and all nuts into ⅔.
Spread surface of cake with this mixture, smoothing all around, leaving center empty.
Fold remaining 4 oz. melted chocolate and chopped glace cherries, into ⅓ cream.
Fill center hole of bowl with this mixture.
Top surface with any leftover cake, this will be bottom when unmolded.
Chill several hours or overnight, (improves) as flavors blend.

Glaze

In a stainless bowl, melt chopped chocolate over simmering water. Spread chocolate out onto parchment into shape of large leaves. When set, peel of parchment and press to sides of cake. Chill. This is easier than it reads. Just try it. Or pour melted chocolate over as a glaze.

22

Rome

After several idyllic days at the Palumbo Palace recovering from jet lag, we negotiated our way in our compact car to Rome. Harold, our wise travel agent, had planned ahead so on our upward journey towards Rome we were on the inside lane of a very narrow, two lane road clinging to the vertical mountainside of the Amalfi coastline. I can't express enough how narrow or scary this road is; it even has mirrors at some of the hairpin turns to warn of oncoming heavy trucks or tiny cars to avoid possible collision.

Our pension in the center of Rome was just as the book described it; "Geraniums spilling over every window box, easy parking and the accommodations inside more than adequate," the travel writer's own words and the right price.

We quickly unloaded our luggage and began to get into the swing of the city. The huge sculpted fountains astounded us right off. How had this civilization created such enormous and dramatic works of art? The leaping cluster of horses and tritons, many times life size, dominate the Trevi Fountain. Pure water flows into the city along the famous aqua duct built years ago during Roman times. Right in the center of this fountain, in a niche, is Oceanus, the god of water being pulled forward in a shell chariot with multi sprays of water spilling over the many basins. The sculpture is a beautiful sight at night under full spotlights.

The famous Spanish Steps were not far from our pension. Artists with their easels, colorful umbrellas shading clustered tubs of flowers scattered over the terraced steps, ended at a spoke of glamorous shops such as Fendi, Missoni, Cartier and Gucci. One afternoon, a sudden storm brought torrents of water gushing down those steps and into the streets below, rendering our shoes so soggy that we were forced into a famous shoe store to purchase new footwear and an Ombrello. It was the Gucci boutique! We ducked into more doorways, somehow resisted spending, then the rain ceased.

Everywhere small Vespas zoomed past us weaving in and around cars and pedestrians. I was careful to hold tightly to my purse, making sure I wasn't a victim of grab and run thieves. No matter, one Vespa almost ran me down, grabbing for my bag but I screamed, "No—No!" holding on tight, swinging my new *Ombrello* at him.

A little out of breath, trembling, I sat on the curb gathering my courage. "I'm fine, really I'm fine." Anton helped me up, he dusted off my jeans and we continued on to purchase two fine sketches of the Spanish Steps from an artist just finishing for the day. A delicious dinner was next on our agenda.

Leaving Rome, we headed to the east coast and spent three days enjoying the small towns and beaches of that area. Halfway to Venice, we needed to stretch our legs so Anton pulled over to a grassy shoulder and we stepped out to the overpowering scent of lavender and something else? Right away I said, "It's fresh Thyme."

Anton grabbed the camera and positioned me at to stand just so, "Right, I've managed to get in the flowering fields behind you, what a great picture!"

23
The Gritti Palace

Approaching the outskirts of Venice, we gave up our car and negotiated our first trip in a Vaporeto, a bus system of small ferry boats for the many canals around the city. Here we were, in Venice, the main reason for my trip.

Cooking Classes were being offered at the famous Gritti Palace that stands on the Grand Canal, just off St Mark's Square. Each morning for a week, I eagerly waited in the palace kitchen with eleven other participants, all from the States except me, from Canada, a novelty. What *trucs* and recipes will we learn? Chef Giovanni Caione gave us his first secret: his personal pasta sauce, made daily for the many dishes on the hotel menu. The *truc* here was canned plum tomatoes! What heresy! I made notes for my proposed classes back home, planning a big build up to the use of canned tomatoes. I said to the others, "I can hardly wait for my students' expressions!" There were many truly fine points to learn about fresh pasta making, Italian fillings and desserts.

Ending the week Chef Caione made a delicious mousse-like dessert called Zabaglione Freddo adding Marsala wine for the authentic flavor. Many variations are possible, using pureed fruits, berries and even chocolate. It's a very showy presentation, whisking egg yolks, sugar and wine in a stainless bowl over simmering water to a fluffy stiffness, then spooning it into champagne flutes. Serve with a crisp biscuit on the side. I made more notes, clustering all the recipes that I could group into six classes back home. The week ended with the presentation of an impressive diploma of attendance with my name on it. It was all so worthwhile.

ZABAGLIONE FREDDO

This is the recipe from the Gritti Palace in Venice. What an elegant, old, prestigious hotel right on the Grand Canal! Think of all the famous people who have sat at that bar, on those stools and sipped icy adult beverages there.

Serves 16
Champagne type flutes
Easy

1½ cups white wine
8 egg yolks
⅔ cup sugar
1 pkg. plain gelatin
⅓ cup cold water
2 cups heavy cream, whipped soft
½ cup Marsala wine or ¼ cup Grand Marnier

Method
Using a metal bowl over simmering water, whisk sugar, wine and yolks until triple in volume.
Set up gelatin in cold water to dissolve grains, then whisk into hot egg mixture to blend. Add Marsala.
Cool in bowl over ice.
Whip cream to soft peaks: add to first mixture chilling briefly to start to set up. Pipe into champagne flutes or wine glasses and chill.
Top with berries (optional), candied violets or whipped cream rosette.

Ps, this is a super, easy, make-ahead finish for a dinner party or catering. If renting wine glasses, transport filled glasses to location in the sectioned rental box.

24
Yugoslavia

While I was at the morning classes at the Gritti Palace, Anton enjoyed the surrounding architecture, shops and small espresso cafes nearby. He had picked out some beautiful glassware from the famous Murano factory boutique. In the afternoon, back at that shop, he showed me all his purchases. "Wow," I said, "How will we get it home?"

"Murano Glass will pack and ship it free, directly to our house in Canada," he said. Anton, temporarily putting aside financial worries, was pleased with himself. He was now having a great time and was gathering his energy to meet all his relatives in Tuçepi. He had been away too long. I could feel the anticipation building.

Anton's prize at the end of my cooking classes in Venice was the gem, Yugoslavia. He had retained his native tongue, remarkably speaking English with absolutely no hint of foreign accent.

The night train from Trieste to the border town of Opatia, was no threat to the glamour of the Orient Express! No sleeping car; merchant sailors with bags of food, wrapped sandwiches and live chickens in baskets kept us enthralled. Anton immediately started to use his county's language. The seamen were surprised when he said he had been away.

"For a month?" they asked.

"No, for forty-five years," he said. They couldn't believe it his Croatian accent was so perfect.

We left the train early in the morning, picking up a pre-arranged car across the Italy border in Opatia. Tuçepi, our final destination was almost in view. Driving down the coast road, past Rjieka, past Split, the beginning of the Adriatic Riviera, we saw the sign for Tuçepi. Turning off the highway towards the beach, we soon found all the relatives waiting. His Aunt Neda and his father's brother, Uncle Reko, welcomed us with tears, open arms and much conversation. I smiled a lot. We had arrived.

This was a wonderful homecoming for Anton. Next morning my husband and I climbed the trail to the old village. He had started his life in a stone hut on the mountain hillside high above the Adriatic. The original hut was still there. The vacant windows open to the winds, allowed straw and weeds over the dirt floor where the donkey would have been. We leaned against the doorway and marveled at how far he had come in his lifetime.

Further along the trail, at another tumbledown rocky dwelling, an old Baba in a typical black kerchief and long, black, shapeless dress, was sitting in front of her doorway. We stopped, she hesitated, then burst out, "Moie Ante, Moie Ante," and clasped him with her shaky arms; she had been waiting a long time to see him again. This was the very woman who had nursed him as a baby, a wet nurse, to help his mother so many years ago. They stood on that stony path, clutching each other, the hot morning breeze drying their tears, the air filled with the scent of pine. Piercing emotion flooded my senses, this moment stood still in time.

Many afternoons we spent with relatives and friends drinking wine, eating crusty bread and snacks of olives and sweets. Of course dinner came later.

Neda's day started before sunrise, with bread in the oven and soup simmering on the stove top. She made wonderful soups and one was always simmering in her kitchen. Each noon day meal always started with some kind of soup, followed with meat, chicken or fish. With my limited phrases, I said, "How do you manage this by one o'clock every day?" It all totally impressed me. Watching and eating was my bonus.

AUNT NEDA'S SOUP

I first tasted this wonderful soup in the small town of Tuçepi, Dalmatia, in the seaside home of my husband's closest relative, his Dad's brother Reko. Neda, Reko's wife, made soup every morning, ready for the one o'clock meal. Always soup of some kind was served first. Fish, meat and vegetables followed to complete the meal. Making a flavorful stock is the key here.

Easy, but lots of ingredients.
Serves 8-10

Chicken stock
6 lb. chicken pieces, wing tips, neck, backs, chopped
3 qts. cold water
3 large onions
2 large carrots, chopped
2 ribs celery, leaves, also, chopped
2 leeks, chopped
1 large turnip, peeled, chopped
1 large onion, unpeeled, whole
½ bunch parsley
2 garlic cloves
1 bay leaf
1 sprig thyme
Salt
½ tsp turmeric

Method

Combine chicken parts and cold water and bring to a boil.
Skim off any foam from surface.
Simmer 2 hours, skimming occasionally.
Add remaining ingredients and simmer 2 hours.
Strain through moistened cheesecloth.
Reduce to about 12 cups liquid.
Stock can be made ahead, cool and refrigerate.

Petite Meatballs

¼ lb. ground beef
½ cup fine dry bread crumbs
½ cup finely minced onion
2 Tbsp. heavy cream
S/p
2 cups torn spinach leaves
1 cup shredded cooked chicken meat.
Form small meat balls with all except spinach and chicken.
Chill.

Final assembly

Heat stock to boil, then reduce to simmer.
Add small meat balls, cook 5 minutes.
Add chicken meat and cook 2 more minutes
Taste for salt, add if necessary.
Tear spinach, add to pot, remove from heat, ladle into bowl
and serve.

25

Cousins

For me the afternoons involved lazing on the smooth pebble beach or swimming in the deep, velvet-blue water of the Adriatic. The water was so clear and salty, thirty feet deep only a few yards from shore. Somehow it was so clean, no algae or seaweed. It was cool and refreshing like a spa.

Anton was kept busy reclaiming his language, reuniting with all the many cousins along the beach. He joined me at the water's edge as the day went on.

One afternoon, when we had been there about eight days, lunch was set out on a long, white draped table under the olive trees. Small bouquets of beach flowers and grasses in glass jars marched down the center of the table. Small rocks anchored the cloth at the ends, keeping the afternoon breezes at bay.

All the cousins, parents and children were laughing, chattering away in Slav as they passed bread, chicken, olives, salamis and cheeses. I encouraged everyone to speak in their language, not to be concerned that I could not join in. Homemade wine kept filling and refilling the glasses. We were getting delightfully drunk. Suddenly, I jumped up and slapped the end of the table.

"Listen, everyone I just understood that whole sentence." I felt very pleased with myself.

One of Anton's cousins proceeded to tell us about a small seaside taverna that offered local specialties. He said, I'll show you where to turn off and drew the directions on a slip of paper to follow the dusty road down to the sea. "They have the best steamed mussels and crepes, anywhere."

It was not quite dark, the sun just setting over the Adriatic when we arrived at the quaint restaurant perched on the edge of the water. A tiny dock jutted into the sea making the location accessible by small boats too. At first we were the only patrons, but soon other diners appeared out of the dusk from the unmarked road above. By the time we had our wine, the place was almost full.

We ordered the house specialties, mussels and Palaschinke. The mussels, called Perstisch were an unusual kind: long and narrow that burrow into the sandstone cliffs at the edge of the water. Sweet and velvety, they were the most delicious morsels, served in a wide bowl, swimming in a delicate broth scented with herbs and their own juices. The crepes were large, thin, pan fried pastries, delicate but crispy at the same time. Grated chocolate and finely chopped walnuts from the local trees, dusted the surface, then the crepes were folded like a fan and served two to a plate with a dollop of heavy whipped cream. Mouth-watering!

CREAM PALASCHINKE (YUGOSLAVIAN CREPES)

*These are the best Palaschinke I have ever eaten.
We were at a small seaside taverna below Tuçepi on
the road to Dubrovnik. These crepes were the house
specialty. It was an exceptional dinner from start
to finish.*

1 Tbsp. sugar
3 Tbsp. soft butter
3 egg yolks
3 egg whites whipped stiff but not dry
1 cup all-purpose flour
½ tsp. salt
1 cup milk
Zest of 1 orange

Method
Beat yolks, sugar and soft butter.
Add flour, salt to blend.
Add milk and last fold in stiff egg whites.
Let rest in refrigerator 1 hour.
Use crepe pan, medium hot, grease each time between crepes with brush of
butter.
Make very thin, edges should be crispy, stack parchment paper.
Continue to cook or freeze.

Filling
1 cup heavy cream whipped
¼ cup walnuts, toasted, ground
¼ cup shaved chocolate

<u>Assembly</u>

Lay crepe flat on large plate, sprinkle with walnuts and chocolate. Add dollop of whipped cream. Fold over into triangle or roll, dust plate with confectioner's sugar. What a special souvenir. Ten days was not enough time in Tuçepi.

We had to depart for the Dubrovnik airport and Vancouver. While waiting in the lounge, a favorite game of ours was picking careers of other passengers. One gentleman nearby looked interesting, dark skinned and handsome with a certain air.

I said, "He looks like a movie producer."

Anton said, "Maybe an artist." While we were guessing, my flowered, straw hat had fallen off the luggage near Anton's foot.

The man in question looked our way, said in English, because he assumed we were American, "Sir, your hat has fallen on the ground." (A jest.)

Picking up on the joke, Anton answered in perfect Croatian, obviously a surprise, he said, "Thank you but of course it is my wife's." Laughs, handshakes and business cards followed and we were immediately travel partners! It turned out he was a well- known local artist with a sense of humor.

I returned to Vancouver with sketches, notes and recipes ripe to assimilate into two series I planned to call Regional Italian and Central European Cooking. This was all new material experienced first-hand, fresh in my mind. So many stories to tell in my next set of classes, I was fairly bursting.

Cuisine de Barbara continued to flourish. Scheduling classes from October to May left time for summer travel and research, marketing and new ideas to weave into each series. The next two summers took us to England, Portugal, Greece and France always ending in Tuçepi. My travel plan was working. However, Anton was still not productively employed anywhere.

I continued to be passionate about my school, no way to turn back, but it still felt like a wonderful hobby. Wearing the title of Cooking School owner rested a little uneasily on my shoulders. A few requests for dinners, desserts and wedding cakes were coming in, so not to turn anything away, I named the offshoot,

The Right Stuff Catering. I thought, "I had a built in clientele from my school."

In my waking hours I produced new classes, and catered events. In my dreams, Anton's financial debacle filled my darkest hours.

26
The Boys

I'm filled with longing as I reflect back to my children and those early homemaking days. It was all still clear in my mind. Three sons so close in age were bound to be competitive, but of course they remained blood buddies.

Each son chose different sports in which to excel. I hoped my efforts during those growing years had a lasting, positive effect. From early kindergarten through high school and university, I was the one who took them on many Sunday trips to Stanley Park: bundling the buggy into the back of the car so baby David could ride while Anthony and Paul held onto the sides as they walked along. Going to the zoo, then a picnic, all this to let Anton sleep undisturbed and eventually go off and play golf with his buddies, was a weekly event. I was completely engrossed with the children.

I drove up the steep Mount Seymour road in North Van to the ski area by six A.M., (I was still concerned with costs at this stage: it was cheaper to ski there than other locations). The parking area still had spaces, so we could easily meet there mid-morning, for a break when we were cold and tired.

All these arrangements needed consideration when small children are involved. This was still the early years. At home, by noon, pulling off snow soggy pants and mitts right into the wash, the boys were ready for lunch and a quiet afternoon. From those first excursions together I learned to ski really well, but the boys soon surpassed me in style and speed.

Our place was always filled with boys after school. Our house was the place to be. The aroma of fresh baked bread swirled through the front door. Warm slices spread with peanut butter plus a plate of chewy cookies set out on my kitchen counter welcomed then all. I supported fund raisers for swim team, soccer, tennis or football no matter what else was on my agenda. The school years slid by.

Anthony loved the rush of skiing and was a daredevil on the slopes. With the station wagon filled with boys, wet jackets, gloves, boots, skis and poles, we passed around sandwiches and hot chocolate on a two-hour drive home after skiing these distant slopes, sharing stories from the day. All the moves you see in the winter Olympics, he and his friends had been doing for years. Hot-dogging, flips and those crazy moguls were just their thing. They had young knees! Now years later, they get dropped off by helicopter to track down untouched powder in the treacherous Bugaboo Mountains in British Columbia.

Paul was a sailing fanatic and had the trophies to prove it. Even when we had acquired a big yacht, he preferred the challenge of the one or two man class. These boats were so quick to respond to any flick of the rudder. He especially liked the "Laser," a one man boat giving him complete control to read the waves and wind, master of his own destiny. He made a makeshift hiking bench to position in front of the TV in our family room. The idea was to lean out from the bench, feet tucked under for position and haul on a rope to imitate heeling, strengthening the stomach and thigh muscles beyond endurance. Paul was always training or away at a regatta, in rain, sun or snow, year round. He parlayed his talent into travels around the world, finally representing Vancouver, Canada in the winter Olympics in Germany.

David, the youngest, was a top student and loved tennis. He practiced at school with the team, and also at the Hollyburn Country Club where we were members. Sometimes he would agree to play singles against me. To tune up my game, to get rid of those "old lady on the back foot" shots, he'd shout, "Step into it, anticipate the ball." Now as I play Pickleball, (a bit like tennis,) I remember his words. David has gone on to be a golf fanatic, using his hand/eye coordination from tennis to good use.

At the high school graduation award ceremony, David's name was called seven times; for scholastic, all around student, by student vote, the French award, the math award, the tennis team group award and more. It was wonderful to sit in that auditorium with our buttons bursting with pride.

There was more to the growing years than just sports, food and studying. Rock concerts were really the thing! All the wonderful new music swept me away just as much as the kids. It was one more chance to bond with my children and be in on their scene. I loved the energy! Vancouver was one of the first cities to showcase all this wild music. I can still visualize and hear Led Zeppelin's *Stairway to Heaven,* The Door's *Light My Fire,* and the Rolling Stones, *Satisfaction.* I get all nostalgic when I hear that music today on a '70's station. I loved it all.

The Miachika's left their mark; not just at the school, they had filled my life with blossoms. Those boyish times would not happen again. They were now out of high school and onto the University of British Columbia, U.B.C.

BARBARA'S CARAMEL/PECAN CHOCOLATE BARS

These bars were a big hit with the after school crowd. Bake and freeze any leftovers in zip lock bags. We took these on ski trips as quick nourishment.
Use 11x17 hotel style sheet pan, makes 30 squares

Easy

Base
1¼ cup flour
¾ cup sugar
1¼ cups coconut
5 oz. soft butter
Spray sheet pan.
Mix well in medium bowl, press with fingers to blend.
Press this base in a thin covering onto sheet pan, pressing flat with fingers.
Bake 10 minutes at 350 set aside

Chocolate Layer
1 pkg. brownie mix, prepare using ingredients listed on box instructions, set aside

Topping
¼ cup melted butter
¼ cup packed brown sugar
1 Tbsp. flour with a pinch of baking powder
¼ cup light corn syrup
1 tsp vanilla

2 eggs
2 cups pecans

Method
Preheat oven 350.
Place brown sugar and flour in medium bowl; stir to blend.
Add corn syrup and vanilla stir in melted butter.
Loosely beat 2 eggs in a separate bowl, add to first mixture.
Stir in pecans.

Assembly
Pour brownie mix evenly over cookie base.
Spoon caramel/pecan mixture over all.
Bake in preheated oven, middle rack for about 25-30 minutes.
Don't over bake.
Let cool, cut into 30 squares, 5 across, 6 long.

27
The Blues Brothers

Joanne, my third hand and special helper at Cuisine de Barbara and catering company, The Right Stuff Catering in West Vancouver, always arrived on time and helped with any challenge. When doing off-premise catering, the first important thing is to arrive on time at the client's location. This was one of my selling points when booking an event. We were reliable.

One such event was set up for a party at an historical mansion in the Shaughnessy district of Vancouver's upscale elite. Impressive mansions simply flooded every romantic, curving, tree-shaded boulevard for eight blocks up and down.

We had already spent hours creating delicious hors d'oeuvres, a buffet spread and meltingly delicious small tarts filled with lemon curd, (homemade of course), fresh raspberries atop frangipane, (a type of almond paste), and chocolate mousse topped with crunched chocolate covered coffee beans. The van was carefully loaded with me handing box after box and trays to Joanne as she stood in the truck, placing each piece securely for the ride over the Lions Gate Bridge to greater Vancouver from our home base here in West Van.

I was wearing large, dark glasses as I had just had eye surgery the day before and used them to cover up my two black eyes with the large frames. I felt comfortable with the disguise. Joanne remarked about it but I just brushed it aside saying, "I am OK. I can see fine."

I had the motor running, while Joanne rushed up the driveway to unlock the iron gates at the top of my property. Swinging over the heavy iron latch with one hand, and bending to lift the pin bar at the foot, she somehow smacked the latch right into her eye, hitting it really hard. Immediately a huge swelling appeared and within seconds, a black eye. We had to continue with our event, the *Show Must Go On*, so we arrived as planned, both sporting dark shades, as if this was our trademark, looking like the Blues Brothers. We appeared quite eccentric, in our checkered chef pants and white jackets. No one questioned our glasses even though it was a dark cloudy afternoon. The catering job proceeded and was well received. Everything was delicious of course.

Joanne said, "No big deal," as we climbed into the van and headed on our way home. *No big deal* was a favourite expression of hers. Whenever Joanne and I touched in over the years, she never failed to remind me of our black eyes and all the fun we had while I was trying to stay alive. She thought it was fun but I remember all the hard work.

ARTISTIC CHEESE STRAWS

Cheese Straws make an artistic statement on a buffet table or a special cocktail party. Stacked upright like Pick-up-Sticks in a mug or crystal container they give height and interest to your presentation. A cluster of radishes still on the stems/leaves, and a mixture of soft butter and feta cheese makes a good accompaniment. I have been making these for many years and everyone always asks, "How do you cut them so fine?" Just say it's your secret.

Oven 425, 7-10 minutes
Parsley cutter/mincer with rolling blades
Medium

1 cup flour
1 cup shredded strong cheddar cheese
1 tsp. dry mustard
1 tsp. salt
1 Tbsp. melted butter
Pinch cayenne
⅓ cup milk or enough to make a stiff dough.

Method
Mix all ingredients and let rest ½ hour in refrigerator.
Roll out under plastic to ⅛" thickness.
Spray sheet pans.
Using cutter, make long strings, stretching them out on pans.

Sprinkle with more salt.
Bake at 425 for about 7 minutes. Watch closely to prevent burning.
Cool on cake rack.

PERFECT CHOCOLATE MOUSSE

Here is the easy chocolate Mousse dessert mentioned in the above catering episode. People are always impressed with anything chocolate and this one is so rich and smooth your mouth will thank you. It's perfect for making ahead and transporting to an event. It's the little finish on top that sells it!

Easy

⅓ cup very hot coffee
1 8oz. package of semi-sweet chocolate chips
4 egg yolks
2 Tbsp. coffee liqueur
4 egg whites

Whipped cream and chocolate covered, crushed coffee beans.

Method
In an electric blender, put chocolate and hot coffee.
Cover and blend to very smooth.
Add egg yolks and liqueur.
Whip whites in separate bowl to stiff peaks.
Fold blender mixture into whites, just until no white remains.
Fill champagne or wine glasses with mousse.
Top with whipped cream and a few crushed chocolate covered coffee beans.

28
Gourmet Getaway

Cuisine de Barbara was part of the new cooking scene in Vancouver. A local West Coast magazine featured my school and some of my recipes. The food editor of our city newspaper, The Vancouver Sun, often called me for ideas regarding seasonal produce.

She'd ask, "What can we say about eggplant, or "Help me describe a great Valentine dessert. I need the recipe and a picture." Their photographer found his way to my West Vancouver school on a regular basis, taking pictures of special desserts and recipes. Each exposure added more students to my roster. I was working hard and getting recognition.

Our local community television station called to see if I was interested in doing a small series of shows? "How would that work," I asked. They sent one camera man and one set of cables and lights and just left the rest up to me.

There I was in my kitchen and he said "You can start anytime."

I plunged in. "Hi, you're' watching Cuisine De Barbara. Join me here in my kitchen to learn about filleting a whole, slippery, Pacific

Salmon." It was pretty hokey but I laughed and smiled up at the camera, while wielding my big chef knife to fillet the fish. Next, "This is how to pull out those pesky pin bones, using small pliers, to give you perfect salmon ready for the grill." I can't remember what was for dessert but something with poached fruit and Crème Anglaise. I liked it! I felt comfortable. The series was a success and the local North Van station ran the series twelve times.

Anton was now briefly excited about the possibility of doing a national cooking show. We could present it together. It could be titled, "Gourmet Getaway." The premise was for us to experience different travel destinations, discover unusual foods common to that area, then return and I would cook it all in my kitchen. A travel show with food! I thought, so perfect. "Maybe it will save us." Well darn, it didn't get off the ground. We had spent about $25,000 to get it this far; everything to do with video-taping, and live photography costs a fortune. The crew comprised at least ten people on location, just to get it on film. Marketing and who you know is still the ticket to success. Anyway, national TV stations in Toronto didn't pick up the pilot and any further financing of ours, dried up. Maybe I wasn't quirky enough to catch any big time producer's attention. Example: Guy Fieri on the Food Chanel is crazy, has weird hair, he is charming in a rough sort of way, over the top.

I see now that current cooking shows have dozens of people to create that perfect image on screen. We were trying to take on too much.

Anton lost interest. I was disappointed but kept busy with my school.

BARBEQUE SALMON

This is one lesson from my little TV series. Fresh Pacific Salmon is one or the most satisfying fish to work with. Look for a clear eye, not slimy skin, and a fresh sea smell,, not strong or overpowering. Filleting and boning can be accomplished after just a few tries. Eating without the trouble of bones is a delight. Just read the recipe all the way through to get the steps of preparation.

One 10 lb. Salmon, gutted, filleted and boned, (skin off optional)
Medium

Marinade and basting sauce
Kosher salt
Fresh coarse ground black pepper
2 Garlic, mashed
Salad oil and butter
Fresh parsley, minced
Fresh dill weed, minced

Method
If you choose to leave the skin on, the salmon can go directly on the hot grill, skin side down.
If skin is removed, use two thicknesses of foil under the fish to aid and preserve the shape as it cooks.
Have the grill very hot.
Marinate the salmon at least one hour, refrigerated, before grilling.

Cut salmon portions on a slant, assembling fish back into original shape.
Lay pieces in order on grill, snugging close together.
Baste as fish cooks.

When fish is opaque ¾ of the way through, remove from heat to a warm platter, cover with foil.
Fish will continue to cook for five more minutes. Serve with lemon and extra minced dill.
Steamed rice and fresh steamed Bok Choy is a nice accompaniment.

29
S-o-o-o Martha

Looking back, my boys were so entrepreneurial. I think they got that talent from me. They were seven, nine and ten.

I made Christmas wreaths for our house. They thought of selling them to our neighbors, up and all around the hill. Soon the mud room was filled with wet cedar boughs, newspaper, decorations and gold paint. We were so Martha Stewart.

Our property had huge cedar and hemlock trees just waiting to be trimmed. It got to be a yearly tradition to supply these works of art, every bit as good as or better than store-bought creations. Neighbors left notes on our door to be sure to get their order in early sometimes as many as three of four wreaths per household. As Christmas got closer, every spare minute was used to wind paper and boughs into wreaths, rolling fine wire all around to secure the decorations. I said, "This is a factory!" The house smelled like a forest, no need for artificial air diffusers.

As the boys got older, in grades ten, eleven and twelve, starting to think more about university, Anthony said, "We should start a painting company. We could call it "The Paint Gang." He employed his own brothers as well as his friends to work during the summer months, lining up houses and commercial prospects for them to paint. It was hard work and sometimes dangerous if they had to use scaffolding, but the profits multiplied. They learned a skill, and how to think ahead.

One year Anthony even had two jobs: he rushed home at four o'clock from the Paint Gang, to change into a Hawaiian shirt to wait tables in a local bar for the evening. The boys had their University fees covered.

Anthony, the oldest, was very artistic. He loved clothes and he was always into the latest styles. It was the flower power years. We were shopping in Gastown, a boutique area of Vancouver, when he saw a deerskin shirt in a window. "Wow what a great shirt, I wonder how much it is?" he said, as we stood there outside the shop.

"Let's go in and see." I said.

Well it was $200 and out of the question. As we walked out I suggested, "I could buy the skins, make the pattern and you could sew it together." So that's what we did. I made the patterns from his designs and he glued and hand sewed them. Jackets, pants and even a long, flowing coat were created.

I was in Gastown shopping and was wearing the hand-stitched, beautiful soft leather pants Anthony had created for me. A complete stranger, a man, looked at me and asked,

"Excuse me, but where did you buy those pants?"

It turned out this man was the buyer for a department store in West Van.

More conversation, "Could Anthony make more of these, and did he have other stuff?" he asked.

Several of the girls at school had him make custom, short, motorcycle style leather jackets. I began to think, maybe Anthony was gay? He really had an eye for style!

Anthony did have a showing at the department store, sold all ten items but decided it was too much hard work so gave it all up. He went back to skiing and football.

Each son went on to The University of British Columbia, Anthony and Paul to graduate with a BA in Economics, and David with a degree in Engineering. David went on to take Law at Dalhousie University in Halifax graduating among the top 3 students and now had two degrees. When I asked him what degree was going to be the direction he wanted to follow, he said,

"I want to be a lawyer able to handle structural, engineering problems." and this is what he did! His plan was a sound one.

They were on their way to the grown up part of their lives. Proud of them? Of course!

30
Marketing

I was immersed in marketing my classes, creating original recipes and complete menus into more complicated programs to entice existing students to return to each new series. Paperwork, testing recipes for timing, and selling the classes person to person or over the phone was hard work but filled my kitchen. To stay ahead, I was constantly researching new trends. As the courses multiplied, I kept a master sheet on each class with notes to myself; timing, improvements in the recipe and presentation décor. I continued to teach, realizing the students were equally important as the food. As a teacher I needed to ensure they absorbed my passion as each new recipe was completed.

Occasionally, Anton offered some financial wisdom, but this did not assuage my misgivings. His former bravado and confidence was gone. He dabbled in a few deals, sold a few more of our stocks, alluded to future plans, but he had lost his drive. Anton was not adjusting well to his loss of position at "Four Seasons." I had always admired his golden touch but where was it now? He wasn't working or creating any new directions. His days were spent in idle hours at the golf club as he reminisced with acquaintances at a favourite drinking haunt overlooking the harbor.

What about a pay cheque? Many evenings he would return home about eight PM while I had a class in progress. Did my students notice if he was a bit unsteady? I would quickly cover for him with, "How was your day? Are you hungry for some dinner? "There will be a plate saved for you when the class is done."

I thought our life will get on track soon. If I keep working hard he will be challenged to find a new direction too. I had already nagged enough, now he had to act.

31
Celebrity Chefs

My school was six years old and I was on a first name basis with many of the influential chefs and restaurant owners in Vancouver. As a member of the IACS, (International Association of Culinary Schools) later changed to I.A.C.P, (Culinary Professionals), and La Chaine de Rotisseures, (a gourmet restaurant and wine group of international note) I felt confident that local chefs would be willing to appear in my kitchen. "Are they taking me seriously?" It was more than a hobby now.

They said, "Yes!" My six lesson series called "Celebrity Chefs" (a new personality each week) was well received as I had a full class each lesson.

One of the first was Michel Clavlin, executive chef at the Vancouver Four Seasons Hotel. Then John Bishop from his own restaurant Bishop's on Twelfth Avenue, in the city.

Umberto Menghi, owner of Umberto's, an Italian restaurant in a well-known little yellow house in downtown Vancouver, (he also owned Il Giardino, and several restaurants at Whistler), was one of the many chefs to make an appearance at my school. One Christmas season, Umberto asked me to create my "Death by Chocolate Log" pastry for his family. This is an enormous chocolate roll, a triple size recipe I had perfected after making it many times. Its' spread with rum flavored chocolate Ganache, sprinkled with crisp chocolate meringue beads, and surrounded with free-form chocolate leaves, topped with truffles and gold leaf.

He said, "Can I pick it up on my way to Whistler on Christmas Eve?" I was flattered he would ask me to make a dessert for this special holiday. I managed to have it boxed and ready for travel.

DEATH BY CHOCOLATE LOG

This is a spectacular chocolate creation, I made for Umberto. I have added thin chocolate waves along the sides of the roll to make it more spectacular. This recipe can be doubled feeding 25. It is a stunning dessert; a real show-off, one you must have in your repertoire.

More difficult
Preheat oven to 375
Use a large mixer bowl
2, 11x17 sheet pans, parchment lined

Serves 16
Oven 375

Cake
1 cup sugar
⅔ cup strong coffee
12 egg yolks
12 egg whites
¾ lb. semi-sweet chocolate, melted

Method
Beat yolks very pale.
Boil sugar and coffee together in small pot for 2-3 minutes producing a hot syrup.
When yolks are beaten, pour syrup down side of bowl over yolks, mixer constantly.
Beat until triple volume.

Remove from mixer and fold in warm melted chocolate. Blend lightly.

Whisk whites until soft peaks, not dry, then fold into chocolate mixture.

Pour and spread onto 2 sheet pans.

Bake only 7-10 minutes. Mixture is quite delicate.

Remove and cool sheet cakes <u>with paper still on.</u>

Filling
2 Tbsp. dry espresso crystals
6 Tbsp. boiling water
1 package plain gelatin
3 cups heavy cream
4 Tbsp. sugar

Method
In a cup, dissolve gelatin, coffee crystals, then boiling water.
Whip cream and sugar, fold into coffee/gelatin mixture.
Spread filling over one sheet cake, adding second cake to surface to add bulk. (Remember to remove paper from second cake.)
Dry chocolate meringue beads can also be added for bulk.
Start rolling from the longest side. Now use paper on the bottom, pulling away as cake is rolled like jelly roll, giving a cake roll 17' long.
Shape and round with hands.
Place in refrigerator to firm up. (it can be made ahead to this point)

Ganache
5 0z semi-sweet chocolate, melted
½ cup heavy cream

2 Tbsp. rum
Un-sweetened baking cocoa
Gold leaf, available in craft stores

Method
Whip cream, add rum and melted chocolate.
Spread over top and sides of roll.
Dust with cocoa.

Touch along the top with pieces of gold leaf. Return to refrigerator

Optional Chocolate Meringue Beads, page 173

Optional finish
Melt 8oz. semi-sweet chocolate. Lay out 2, 6'x17' pieces of parchment on sheet pan.
Spread chocolate in a wavy motion down the length of each paper, making the bottom straight and the top edges wavy.
You now have two bands of thinly spread chocolate.
Place in refrigerator to firm up.
When firm, take paper and chocolate and press against length of log, chocolate against cake, paper on outside. Leave paper on until ready to present on platter or cake board.
Paper will peel away quite easily.
Present with clusters of sugared grapes and maybe a few chocolate truffles.
Add a piece of gold leaf.

Flo Braker, another of my special chefs, author and respected baking specialist from San Francisco, agreed to teach several classes which we simply called, "Baking with Flo Braker." She is a delightful person and a superb teacher; I met her at the I.A.C.P. food conference the year before. One of her books, *The Simple Art of Perfect Baking*, is a reliable reference for anyone, beginner or professional. This was the class for ardent bakers looking for professional tips. I have incorporated many techniques from her books and classes, adding these finishing touches into my own repertoire.

FLO BRAKER'S FRAISIA, STRAWBERRY DOME CAKE

Flo Braker had all the baking techniques we wanted. A very good teacher, she made it all look very easy. Here is a spectacular cake using a few interesting methods for shape and assembly. It's these professional touches that make a difference.

Medium

Basic Sponge Cake, 8"
Use your favorite recipe for the cake baking on a sheet pan
Cut 3 circles of cake; one 8" one 6' one 5". Set aside.

Filling
¼ cup strawberry preserves
1½ cups heavy cream
1 Tbsp. sugar
1 tsp. vanilla
2 oz. white chocolate, grated fine
2½ cups fresh strawberries, (20-30)

Decoration
7 oz. marzipan (=1 lb.)
Green food coloring, 2 drops
Cornstarch
Royal icing
⅓ cup water
2 Tbsp. corn syrup
1 cup sugar

Assembly

Place first circle on a cake board. Spread with thin layer of preserves to edge.

Top with second layer. Whip cream, sugar, vanilla to soft peaks then fold in white chocolate.

Spread ⅓ over cake.

Cover this with berries, tips up.

Add 5" cake layer. Cover with ⅓ more cream, and more berries.

Stopping 1" from edge, add last of cream. Round off with more berries, creating a dome top. Smooth and press cream to cover berries around and on top, pushing cream in and over berries to cover. Refrigerate.

Finnish

Roll marzipan to ⅛" thick on cornstarch dusted surface. Make a circle approximately 14." Brush off excess cornstarch.

Drape over rolling pin. Hold over cake. Unroll. Smooth surface with hands to eliminate wrinkles, working like fondant. Press edges against cake board. Cut clean at bottom edge.

Use scraps of marzipan to make 2 long ropes to drape over top in a crossing fashion.

Place a single berry on top. Chill.

When ready to serve, let come to room temp.

For Royal Icing to write Fraisia

Mix 1 cup icing sugar, 2 Tbsp. egg white.

Pinch of cream of tartar.

Mix all together. Whip until smooth. Use fine tip in piping bag.

32

A Week with Jacques and then Marcella

I had an inspired idea! Long distance phone calls and correspondence to Jacques Pépin, the internationally famous French Chef, teacher, television personality and author, resulted in his promise to teach and cook for one whole week at my school. Several years before, I had been a student in one of his classes in San Francisco, and now hoped to share him with my students. He had never been to our city before so it would be a first! It was 1984

He answered his own phone at his house in Connecticut. *"Ello,"* he said in his delightful French accent.

I stumbled when I realized it was Jacques himself, expecting a secretary to answer, but regained my voice, introduced myself, and laid out the plan I was proposing. Was he interested?

"Of course I am, you know," he said in his own French way. "Send all the information to my secretary and we will do it!"

Without him knowing it, Jacques had become my mentor as I eagerly devoured all the pictures and techniques from his early books, *"La Technique"* and *"La Methode"* To host someone of this caliber was a very expensive undertaking, but he had never taught in Vancouver before, so it was bound to sell out! My students were thrilled to have such a star here in our town and in my kitchen. This series sold out with the speed of a rock star concert.

The event strained all my organizational skills. I had twenty-four students twice a day with notebooks and cameras ready to catch his every nuance. Jacques expected the best quality of everything; he was very much a star, a flirt, in his French way, but still professional.

I shopped for the most perfect everything; Saddle of lamb, Chinatown chickens still warm, wild, slippery, northwest salmon, fresh, pink, spotted shrimp, farm berries, plump and ripe, and flats of fresh herbs still on the roots. By the end of the first morning's class, Jacques had used up some of the ingredients that were supposed to last into the afternoon set! I had to rush out between sessions to buy more. "Help, I told myself, just buy it and worry about the extra cost later."

Local wine representatives, as a free bonus to me, presented their most interesting vintages to go with each food. Each rep. gave all the inside information about the grapes used; the holding time for maturation plus the code to look for, for the sweet or dryness. It was great exposure for them and good information for us. The series was a huge success, a lot of work but rewarding, so we did it again in 1985, the next year for a successful second visit.

One enthusiastic student said, "Barbara, if I get some good close-ups I'm going to make a photo booklet for you." And she did.

Marilyn got every step, and I still have that amazing album on my bookshelf.

Jacques Pépin and Barbara at Cuisine de Barbara
Cooking School in Vancouver, Canada

FROZEN SOUFFLÉ À L'ORANGE AU COGNAC.

This was one of Jacques delicious desserts. I used this recipe as part of a buffet when entertaining the TV crew from Australia.
Serves 8–10

Easy

Purchased lady fingers, about 12
Use a five cup glass or attractive, round serving bowl.

½ cup plus 3 Tbsp. sugar
¼ cup water
1 Tbsp. zest of orange
4 egg yolks¾ cup Grand Marnier
2½ cups heavy cream, whipped
12 ladyfingers
1 Tbsp. unsweetened cocoa

Method
In a saucepan, combine sugar, water and zest of orange.
Bring this mixture to a simmer, to create a syrup, about
3 minutes.
Beat egg yolks slightly in a mixer bowl and pour stream of hot syrup onto inside of bowl, into yolks, beating at high speed for about 10 minutes or until mixture forms a ribbon when beater is lifted, and it thickens.
Pour ½ cup brandy in a stream beating about 3 minutes,
Mixture will still be thick.
Fold the whipped cream with a spatula.

Pour remaining brandy into a shallow dish. Lightly dip ladyfingers in brandy.

Pour ⅓ of mixture into mould.

Arrange 6 ladyfingers over surface.

Pour additional ⅓ mixture over to use bring mixture ⅔ way up bowl.

Arrange last 6 fingers over surface.

Pour more soufflé mixture to the top of bowl. You should have about 2 cups mixture left.

Refrigerate bowl and left over mixture.

Tie a 2-3" collar around bowl. Add remaining mixture, freeze all overnight or until frozen.

Dust with cocoa, remove collar.

During my European travels, I had taken a week of classes at Marcella' Hazan's internationally renowned school, Marcella Hazan Italian Cuisine, in Bologna, Italy. I arrived by train into Bologna's station just days after the Red Brigade, a revolutionary group, had blown it up. Not to be deterred, I kept to the plan for her class and felt it wouldn't happen twice in the same place! The sessions included field trips and special restaurants on the nearby river, (I can't remember the names).

I wondered if Marcella might agree to visit Vancouver. I did name drop that Jacques Pépin had already appeared. I knew she was friends with Jacques and moved in the same circles. She looked at her calendar. "A big "sì, grazie." She agreed to do a week in Vancouver for her next season's schedule.

Marcella and Victor Hazan agreed to teach classes in November and their appearance was a gem. Vancouver was a first for this International duo. Marcella is a well-known teacher and author, "The Classic Italian Cook Book," and later, "More Classic Italian Cooking." Her husband, a charming and elegant counterpoint and wine expert, was also supported with his book, "Italian Wine." Many years later, their son Guiliano, who lives in Tampa, Florida, has picked up the gauntlet and teaches there.

My students watched intently as Marcella described the differences between fresh and dried pasta and when to use each. She was all business and perfection. Marcella made it all look easy. She held up a 4 inch square of fresh pasta and showed, "This is how to shape Tortellini." Then she described the different shapes of Maltagliati, Quadrucci and Fettuccine. Victor was a delightful foil as he described the virtues of Italian wines and the Italian country side of their homeland. They finished the series with an unusual dessert made with Vanilla Ice cream, powdered espresso coffee and Scotch.

GELATO SPAZZACAMINO, VANILLA ICE CREAM POWDERED ESPRESSO COFFEE AND SCOTCH

This surprising combination came from Marcella Hazan when she was teaching at my school in West Vancouver.
Grind the coffee very fine and keep in a separate container for future use. This was a favourite and fun dessert that everyone loved.

Easy

For each serving
2 scoops vanilla ice cream
2 tsp dry espresso coffee, ground very fine to a powder
1 Tbsp. Scotch whisky

Method
Put 2 scoops ice cream in individual shallow bowl.
Sprinkle coffee powder over.
Add Scotch as suggested, quantities up to your taste.

33
Wes and David

With each new personality, the press gave me a generous review, sometimes a whole sheet on the Vancouver Sun food page, featuring pictures and many of the recipes. The more credibility I garnered, the moodier and more vacant Anton became. The summer trips abroad had temporarily revived him, but each September he fell into a gloomy pit, not working or creating any income. He became noticeably abusive. His tirades were becoming all too frequent, prompted by his drinking in the safety of an empty, darkened kitchen. I was the one he dumped on, flinging all his insecurities down the hall to the bedroom. I was awakened night after night; he would rip the sheets and quilts off the bed, forcing me to get up to listen to his ranting, then I would try to reason with him, grabbing the bottle and pouring the scotch down the bar sink, but to no avail.

I thought, will he turn the corner and stop drinking; if he loses all my respect and the children's also, will he hit bottom, then reclaim our life together? Could my friends and students see how bad it was? I was frantic with worry.

My personal life continued to rush downward in an ever swirling vortex! The boys were living on campus, only at home sporadically now, so they were spared some of my agony. Years later, when I was living with Anne in San Francisco, watching a T.V. program with Farah Fawcett in "A Burning Bed," I finally realized I had also been a battered housewife!

The neighborhood was showing curiosity and interest in all the school activity at my house. Calls regarding the buzz about my classes, how much they cost, what was involved, happened more often now. The Vancouver Sun Newspaper's weekly food column plus wonderful action photos, National Television and Radio segments with pumped up exposure featuring live camera and talk show patter was invaluable. I was excited about every bit of PR.

Next door, my new neighbors, David and Wesley stopped over to formally introduce themselves. David signed up for the evening Italian series, six classes, one a week. He was the owner of David Charles, a boutique hair salon downtown that pampered clients with silver tea service, a relaxing fireplace and down couches while waiting for their 'New You' hair appointment. Très Chic. He knew how to market!

David was front and center for several of my classes, quite a ham but a fun addition to the evening group. We were now quite good friends.

Many nights Anton's demeaning, loud and angry voice escaped out onto the driveway spilling over the nearby property. I know Wes and David could hear us but they didn't mention it. I had given up being embarrassed. Wesley, a psychiatrist, was a professional friend at the right time and knew I needed support. I felt lucky to have their friendship, offered so sincerely and thoughtfully.

I spread my energy between current obligations; catering, classes, financial worries and the prospect of Anthony and Victoria's wedding.

34
Weddings

I knew from the start that, having all boys, I would never realize that special experience of being the Mother of the Bride. I would miss the thrill of being part of the excitement and flurry of planning to realize a daughter's hopes and desires for such a special day. I would never sit in a bridal salon and say, "That is such a fabulous dress, it is really you," or, "This is the one," the two of us hugging and crying together over all the tiny details. I had boys. They married in chronological order, Anthony, the oldest, was first.

Over the years, Anthony had dated several very interesting girls. This time there was a real excitement to his phone message that he was going to be home around seven PM and wanted us to be there to meet his girlfriend.

Even though each girl was special, I found out the hard way not to get too attached, too soon. This had happened when Anthony and Stacy were anointed "The Couple" of the graduating high school class. Stacy, a darling blonde girl, was easy to love. However, as they progressed on to University, they broke up, each going off to different careers. I think it was as hard on me as it was on Anthony. I warned myself, "Do not get too attached again."

Anthony and Victoria met on a blind date. He was just out of a relationship, and so was she. Can you imagine, I said, "Two such desirable people on the loose." It does happen, the timing was right.

They were smitten from the first date, and before long we heard the words engaged and marriage. I could now truly hug this future daughter-in-law and exclaim, "How excited we are, so thrilled for you and welcome into our family.

Victoria was petite; dark, shiny hair, beautiful dark eyes and perfect teeth, unblemished complexion, wonderful figure and just all-round fabulous. Stylish and well educated, Polish/Italian background, she was fluent in four languages. I was excited for them both. I took Anthony aside and whispered, "Good going, Anthony!"

When it came time to think about the actual wedding, the obvious reception choice was the prestigious Capilano Golf and Country Club of which Anton was a member. He knew the staff and players from years of membership, spending many hours on the course and at the 19th hole. The façade of business executive was still his image and he easily arranged the financial details to have the wedding reception there. This was still his forte.

I wanted to offer to make the wedding cake. This could be my contribution from our side of the family. How would our bride-to-be feel about that? Would she be reluctant to express ideas of her own, with me, this expert chef soon to be her mother-in- law? I needn't have worried. To my amazement, she wanted me to create her cake. She showed me pictures from books and I said, "Yes, I can make that." As we talked, our ideas came together and the picture of her dreams came to life on paper. It never occurred to me that I would have difficulty. I was so confident, ready to take on this challenge.

In Canada and Europe, family recipes for fruitcake, dark or light were the traditional choice for wedding cakes. I asked them, "Do you want a fruitcake or a genoise (sponge cake) style." Together they decided on the traditional. I began to prepare for the process of enlarging my recipe and planning for the ingredients. The cooking school was in full speed mode so creating a wedding cake so precious seemed just part of my day. When the time came to bake and store this creation, I had plenty of freezer space and cool pantry shelves to easily accommodate all the layers. Three square and two round pans of descending sizes had to be assembled, greased, floured, parchment paper inside, all around, ready and waiting for the batter.

On baking day, mounds of dried fruit filled my biggest bowls; flour, unsalted butter, sugar, cream, nuts, spices and flats of eggs were spread out over all my counters. Brandy, vanilla, and rose flower water would scent the mixture. One of my assistants came in the kitchen and said, "Wow, what are you doing, this looks like Willi Wonka?"

The butter had to be creamed in my extra-large mixer, adding the sugar created a fluffy consistency, then the eggs and spices. I stirred and tossed the fruit and nuts with some of the flour, setting it aside. The dry ingredients were stirred in with a big wooden spoon, alternating with lemon and orange juice, marmalade, finally adding the brandy, vanilla and orange flower water last. My workshop smelled wonderful and the cakes weren't even in the oven yet!

Delicious aromas filled the kitchen. After baking several hours the cakes were removed from the big oven, cooled on racks, wrapped in brandy soaked cheesecloth and set to mellow in the cool pantry for several weeks. As I picked up ingredients from the shelves for daily classes, I patted the pans as if I was giving a blessing, saying, "Rest well and taste perfect for the wedding day."

In night-time dreams I pictured how it would all come together. I had a clear vision of the finished confection, I could see it all.

The multi-tiered cake spread with white butter cream icing, stood decorated with pink icing roses. The sides draped with royal icing ribbon string work and real white satin ribbons cascading down from a tip-top basket. It was as clear as real life.

The wedding was a blur of excitement and happiness. Victoria was a spectacular bride, a vision from 'Vogue,' and Anthony was of course 'GQ' handsome.

The golf club was a majestic setting for the reception. A sit-down dinner, music and toasts to the lucky couple, plus the cake, it was everything Victoria had imagined. Both families had done their best to launch our precious offspring into their married life.

I exhaled, finally relaxing as the last guests left the premises. Anton had conducted himself perfectly even through all the drinks and toasts. His image was intact to the outside world. For me, the cake had created common ground; I had put my best foot forward with my new daughter-in-law.

MASTER WEDDING CAKE RECIPE NO. 1

This was the traditional wedding cake recipe I used for Anthony and Victoria's wedding. Traditional Fruit Cake plus almond paste, snow white butter cream and Royal icing. There are a lot of ingredients but do not be turned off by that. It all works out beautifully.

Oven 250, slow baking.
14" 10" 6" square or round pans, (see end note for more quantity.)
Decorative cake boards, supports and pillars, icing roses or fresh flowers.
Medium

Cake
1½ lb. citron
¾ lb. orange peel
¾ lb. lemon peel
6 oz. candied ginger
3 lb. seedless raisins
1½ lb. currants
1½ Muscat raisins, large, flat and sticky
¾ lb. glace cherries
¾ lb. pecans
6 fresh lemons
1½ cups of marmalade
2 tsp. Vanilla
1½ tsp. lemon extract
¾ cup fresh lemon juice
¾ cup orange juice
½ small bottle rose water, (2 oz.) from specialty store

6 cups flour
1 Tbsp. cinnamon
1½ tsp nutmeg, salt and baking powder, each
1½ tsp mace, cloves, allspice, each
1½ lbs. butter
18 eggs
3 cups sugar

Method
Part 1
Use processor to chop, (in small batches) citron, orange and lemon peel.
Add ginger.
Place all in large stainless bowl- add raisins, currants, cherries, and chopped pecans.
Mix well.
Add grated rind of lemons, marmalade, Vanilla and lemon extract rose water.
Pour juices over fruit. Mix with hands, cover bowl and let rest in warm place overnight. All liquid should be absorbed.

Pans
Line pans on bottom and sides with double thickness of brown paper, (oiled or Crisco).

Part 2
Sift flour, spices, baking powder. Cream butter and sugar to a fluffy consistency, (so sugar is not grainy to the fingers).
Add 18 eggs, one at a time, beating well.
Ass dry ingredients gradually to creamed mixture, add fruit.
Mix with wooden spoon or hands.
Place pan of hot water on floor of oven, place cakes in lower ⅓ of oven.

Fill pans to within 1" of top, if necessary cover largest pan
with foil and refrigerate until other cakes are baked. If you
have two ovens, of course bake all at once.
Timing is approximately 4-5 hours at 250 for 6 and 10" cakes.
Do not over bake.
12"cake might be 6 hours.
Allow to rest ½ hour to cool, then turn out onto cake rack to finish.
Peel off paper, cover loosely with tea towel and let rest
overnight.
Soak cheese cloth in Brandy, wrap cakes, over wrap in foil and
store in cool place for 2-4 weeks.

Almond Paste
Basic recipe
2 lb. almond paste
8 egg whites
1½ boxes confectioner's sugar, (each box =11 cups)
2 tsp. vanilla or rum

Mix together.
Use mixture to cover cake tops and sides.

Method
Roll out on cornstarch dusted surface to ⅛" thick.
Brush tops of cakes with apricot puree then invert onto
almond paste, cut carefully around and invert upright. Puree
will act like glue for paste.
Do the same for sides. The cakes are now enclosed in paste
ready to accept the final icing.

Snow White Butter Cream Icing
⅔ cup water
4 tb meringue powder

1¼ cups Crisco
¾ tsp salt
¼ tsp. butter flavouring
1½ tsp. almond flavouring
½ tsp. vanilla flavouring, (the clear type)
1 box sifted confectioner's sugar, (11 cups)

Method
Combine water and meringue powder to a clean mixer bowl.
Add 4 cups confectioner's sugar, one at a time, beating well
on low speed. Alternately add Crisco and remaining sugar
and flavorings.
This icing keeps well in refrigerator, covered for several weeks.
Recipe yields about 8 cups.
Do x two for tiered cakes.

Tips
For string work add 2 tsp corn syrup for each cup of icing, or
make royal icing.
Color icing in small cups, i.e. pink, or pale green for leaves.
Make ahead and freeze leaves etc.
Coat all surfaces of cakes with a thin crumb coat of icing
over-night, before finishing. Then apply final coat assuring a
perfect, smooth finish.
Top with bride and groom, or a small basket with ribbons and
icing flowers.

To produce 14, 10, 8 and 6 plus 1 one 12" slab, make two
times the recipe

35
L'Ecole Lenôtre

My dessert obsession continued. I was reading a magazine article describing a famous pastry chef, Gaston LeNôtre, the French pastry king. It's a weird sensation when information jumps off the page into your consciousness, forcing thoughts into your inner mind. A new travel scheme formed and before any time at all, plans were solidified. The LeNôtre Pastry School in Paris might be my last trip abroad, but it would be the plum! Our financial worries continued to hover, but I needed to be part of LeNôtre's pastry world. The money would come from somewhere, I was forever optimistic.

Even though French is the official second language in Canada, I was not fluent. Victoria, my new daughter-in-law was accomplished in French and Italian. She agreed to go with me to France and together we would take the classes. She was excited and said, "Yes, what a great opportunity." I thought, "What a *honneur* that she would consider going to France with her mother-in-law." My world was spinning faster than our universe.

Off we went, Victoria, my husband and I. Again, Anton was a great traveler and looked forward to the trip. We had arranged to stay in a flat rented through a contact of Victoria's, right in the center of Paris.

We set the alarm for 4.30 AM, getting up in pre-dawn darkness, preparing for the first day of classes. It was going to be a strenuous week. First of all it was costing me $3000 for the classes for two of us. I wanted to catch every word and nuance from the instructor and my daughter-in-law would be my private interpreter.

Anton waved good-by and mumbled sleepily "Good luck," from his cozy pillow in the darkened apartment. Victoria and I ran down the damp, foggy streets to a pre-arranged pick up location taking us to Plaisir, the town just outside Paris where the LeNôtre headquarters and school was situated. We were really in Paris; peeking into the basement windows, set ajar, letting the aroma of fresh rising croissants and baguettes waft into the street. I said, "Victoria, look down through that lighted window at that baker covered with flour and sweat, pulling out a sheet of *"frés Pain au Chocolat."* It was a surreal moment.

When we arrived, men were mingling in the class workshop. French men in *Toques(* tall chef hats.) We quickly scanned the room to make sure we were in the right place; we were the only women! Everyone spoke French of course. They looked us up and down as if, "What are you doing here, you housewives." In French they laughed, calling us, "The Canadian Spies!" How dare they, we were all paying the same money to be here. The joke was on them however as Victoria had not let on that she was fluent in French and understood every haughty and rude word. We smiled, continued to speak English. The room was tense, waiting for the day to start.

The professor referring to me as Madame Miachika, (not Mrs.), speaking always in French during his remarks, looking about the room, talking about ingredients, suddenly resorted to English saying, "baking powder" in a comical tone, I guess for my benefit? On the next day, he suspected that Madame Miachika was a serious student but tested me with what he thought a tough assignment. Facing me he said, "Take your chocolate and make long ruffles," I sprang into action, this was something I was good at. I produced perfect chocolate ribbons. Everyone applauded. I had gained their confidence. Victoria spoke to them in French and they were surprised and embarrassed. The week ended with a flourish taking a classic snapshot showing everyone in *Toques*, even me. We were all spies together!

The whole experience made me think of Julia Child and her determination to get her degree at Cordon Bleu.

Each evening, Anton had lined up 'must see' destinations for shopping and dining. As tired as we were, somehow, with a shower and a quick sip of adult refreshment, the three of us explored Paris by night. When the week was over, Tuçepi, Yugoslavia was our next resting place and final destination.

The LeNôtre *Entremets* (dessert) Course gave me valuable professional recipes and techniques; how to construct many cakes, fillings, creams and mousses that were reliable, décor touches so different from the norm and endless yarns to add drama to my future dessert classes and cake demonstrations. Like Julia, I now had a prestigious degree!

Victoria, Gaston LeNôtre and Barbara in France

LENÔTRE CONCORD GATEAU,/ CHOCOLATE MERINGUE

This dessert is from my time at the famous LeNôtre Pastry School in France. Three crisp discs of descending size, with a mound of chocolate mousse spread between them to create a dome, looking like half an egg.
Sounds quite complicated but most can be prepared ahead of time.
This (chocolate mousse), is impressive as a separate dessert by itself, and can be scooped with a large spoon from a bowl. I was in the inner sanctum of pastries and loving every sugar crusted piece of pastry.

Serves 10
Oven 275, a separate in oven guide is handy for accurate temp.
Pastry bag and 2 plain nozzles
Medium

Chocolate Meringue
10 egg whites or ¾ cup
7Tbsp. baking cocoa
2 cup confectioner's sugar
1⅓ cups granulated sugar

Method
Preheat oven to 300°, then turn to 275 to bake. Grease and flour 2 baking sheets. Mix cocoa powder with icing sugar and sift.

Beat egg whites until firm, (about 5 minutes). Adding 3 tb granulated sugar while beating. As soon as whites are stiff, add remaining sugar, on low speed.
With spatula, fold in cocoa mixture.

Draw 3 ovals on parchment for cookie sheets 5½ x10 inches, 5 x 8 and making the third a bit smaller as this will be the descending top of dome. Turn paper over placing pencil side down.
Use a pastry bag with plain nozzle, 1 inch size and pipe all 3 ovals into flat disks as above. Use the rest of the meringue to pipe long ribbons on a cookie sheet using ½ inch nozzle.
Bake at 275° for 1 hour and 5 minutes. Check color, don't let get too brown but dry. Ribbons will bake first, then check ovals.
Remove to cool, cut ribbons into 2 inch logs, save into zip lock bag. Can all be made ahead.

Chocolate Mousse
10 oz. semi-sweet chocolate chips
2½ sticks unsalted butter (10 oz.) room temp.
6 egg yolks
8 egg whites (1 ⅓ cups)
10 tsp. granulated sugar

Method
Melt chocolate over hot water
Remove from heat and stir in butter.
Add eggs one at a time. Set aside briefly.

Whisk whites until stiff, adding sugar gradually. Add a little of whites to chocolate mixture to lighten, then fold all chocolate into whites. Don't over mix.
Set to chill ½ hour.

Final Assembly
On attractive large serving platter or silver tray, place bottom disk, spread ⅓ of mousse.
Add second disk, add ⅓ mousse.
Add last disk, spread all mousse over all to make a dome.
Use 2 inch logs to sprinkle over all, top and sides. Refrigerate at least one hour.
Lay a 2 inch wide ribbon of parchment over top, dust with icing sugar. Remove ribbon.
Refrigerate several hours or over-night to firm up.

Barbara J Miachika

Fabulous Chocolate Cake with Chocolate Fans

CHOCOLATE CHANTILLY CAKE WITH CHOCOLATE FANS

This is a show stopper and delicious too. It takes a bit of practice for the fans, but once mastered it will be a great technique to add to your skills. When at the LeNôtre School in Paris, I was able to impress the professor of my ability to manipulate the chocolate sheet with a palate knife. He said, "I see that Madame Miachika has had practice with this already. All you other students take notice" I was in.

Medium

9" spring form
Serves 8
Oven 350

4 egg yolks
4 egg whites
2 Tbsp. water
⅔ cup sugar
1 envelope vanilla sugar
6 drops of bitter almond extract, (Oetker)
¾ cup sifted cake flour
2 Tbsp. cocoa, heaping
2 Tbsp. cornstarch
1½ tsp. baking powder

Method
Grease and line a 9' spring form pan bottom only. Position oven rack in the middle.

In a small mixer bowl beat egg yolks, water and sugar to light.
Add vanilla sugar and bitter almond extract.
Sift flour, cocoa, cornstarch and baking powder onto sheet of parchment.
Fold dry ingredients into egg mixture.
Beat whites in large mixer bowl until stiff but not dry.
Stir one spoonful of whites into main mixture to lighten it.
Fold in rest of whites carefully and blend.
Pour into ready pan, bake at 350 for 35 minutes or until light pressure springs back.
Cool on rack. Slice horizontally into 3. Set aside

Rum Butter Cream, (can be doubled)
⅔ cup sugar
4 egg yolks
½ cup boiling milk
¾ lb. unsalted butter, soft
3 Tbsp. rum

Method
Beat yolks and sugar in small mixer bowl.
Beat in hot milk.
Pour into clean saucepan, over medium heat stir until mixture thickens to light cream.
At once place custard in bowl of ice and whisk to barely warm.
Place back in bowl and whisk in butter by tb until thick and homogenous. Add flavouring.
Cool.
Ponge cake surfaces with simple syrup and rum.
Spread each layer with butter cream, then stack and finish top and sides also.

Chocolate Finish

12 oz. semi-sweet chocolate, chopped fine. In a stainless bowl, melt chocolate over hot water to smooth texture.
Wipe bottom of chocolate pot with a tea towel to prevent water drips as you work.
Use the back clean face of a sheet pan, spread chocolate over surface quite thinly. Allow to set up only long enough to be able to resist finger prints. With a wide stiff metal spatula, mark off 4 inch ribbons, then scrape down sheet creating fans. Place fans on parchment and chill. Add to top of cake. Dust with icing sugar. Practice!

36
Despair

The hour was getting desperate for me. My husband had succumbed to Alcoholism and his abusive behavior escalated. I was really starting to fear for my life. He had never physically hit me, yet, but he spewed out a psychological war of demeaning words grinding me down. Each day that he was non-productive, it just ate away at him. But he failed to save himself, failed to adjust to his financial situation. His ego would not allow him to start over. He pretended to be busy, in his own shadowy world.

I felt helpless. In the mid-night hours, we screamed at each other. Me, desperately pushing him to clarify our financial situation and he, drunk, just shrugged off all responsibility. I was still his wife, under his thumb! I thought people in controlling situations like this were only in the movies or in slums, not me. I threatened to call the police, but he just said, "Go ahead, they won't believe you, they'll think you are just a hysterical, pampered British Properties wife out of control," So there I was, the police responded to my call for help, but when they arrived Anton controlled the scene, he was the professional one. They believed him, not me. They turned and left the scene, not wanting to get involved in our domestic crisis. I didn't know where to turn. It was so unfair and I felt desperate.

37

Bon Appétit Magazine

As I wrote down my thoughts, I looked for the pivotal point in my life: everyone has one. I know there is a power over us, un-seen but present. I'm sure a cluster of angels, feeling my desperation, must have hovered over me while I answered the phone one day in January 1985. Lifting the receiver I said, "Hello, Cuisine de Barbara, may I help you." I was expecting a request for a class or catering.

A voice said, "This is the editor of Bon Appétit Magazine. I understand you have a cooking school and you teach Yugoslavian Cuisine. We hope to feature that style of food in an upcoming issue. We work quite far ahead, so this article wouldn't come out until next March, 1986 a year from now."

I was brimming with excitement and the flattery of being called, rather than calling, it was music to my ears. A feature article in an international magazine would be incredible exposure. My passion for food and all things culinary was paying off.

I gathered my thoughts and quickly confirmed that the style and food specialties of the Mediterranean were very familiar to me.

The Croatian coast had been my travel destination the last three summers. "Yes," I said, "I do teach a series called The Cuisine of Yugoslavia. I featured cabbage rolls, fresh pasta, pot roast with oven roasted garlic and dumplings, many desserts, tortes and my hand-pulled dough for apple strudel."

How had she found my school here in Canada? It had to be my recent connection with Jacques Pépin and his exciting week at my school. He must have been impressed with what he saw here. He had possibly alerted the editor of the magazine about my school here in West Vancouver. My angels' hands were guiding her to me. Now it was up to me to sell myself. My heart was pumping. I was so excited.

There were many phone calls and correspondence back and forth. Testing, planning and staging to verify the recipes and the order of preparation for the photography team were agreed upon. I had seven months to prepare. The magazine shoot was to take place in August 1985 over a two-day period right here in my kitchen. A wedding was already on my calendar for that week-end, the mother of the bride was one of my cooking school devotees. That catering would have to work around the magazine, as I already had the bride's deposit and gave her my word that I would personally be on site to present the food and cut the cake. I'll just hire more staff.

38
Letting Go

Could I hold it all together until the magazine shoot in the summer? Maybe all the confusion in my personal life was about to change for the better; like so many women, I was always ready to forgive, to make it work!

I had tried to keep Anton at arm's length with a restraining order but I didn't hold much faith in it. Our house was secluded from the street with many windows and places for him to hide on the property. I even changed the locks.

I was abruptly awakened about mid-night. Banging and shouting was coming from the kitchen. From my darkened bedroom, I nervously walked down the hall into the bright lights of a flood-lit kitchen. He had managed to get in. He was standing right in my kitchen. Anton, holding an empty glass, was leaning at a rakish angle, peering into my empty file cupboard. What was he doing? At first he ignored me, then sweeping his hand up and over in a Musketeer's flourish, he pointed first to the vacant office shelves, then towards the cul-de-sac at the top of the driveway.

In my pajamas and bare feet, I ran out to the darkened drive-way, up the curve to the cul-de-sac. Even before reaching the top, I could see a bonfire, flames sending sparks high into the night sky. I stood stunned and speechless, let out an anguished sob and sank to the concrete. All my master cooking class files with side bar details, recipes, menus, sketches and notes were being destroyed. Everything I had worked so hard to create and organize was burning. My Rolodex client list, everything. It was too terrible. What a vicious act! Uncontrolled tears were spilling down my face.

I screamed at him, "Get out of here. Get out of our house now, yes, now!" His eyes glazed over. With wild, drunken laughter he sneered into my face, attempting to elicit a desperate reaction. He lunged at me, his fingers gripping my neck…I jerked away, terrified; I had to save myself. His outlandish and deranged actions seemed beyond help. This was definitely the end! I held my breath.

I had tried all I knew to reclaim him. With all this drama, life continued to ebb and flow around me; my classes continued and only a few close friends knew the strain I was under.

39
Wedding No. 2

Paul and Julie were the next to get married. They asked to have their wedding reception at our home. My personal life was precarious but I was still in our house, the bank had not made a final move yet. It would be less expensive and financially sensible to host the reception here. We had the perfect setting for a large affair, maybe one hundred guests. I would be able to produce a feast for all their guests from my professional kitchen. Energetic as usual, I excitedly planned an elaborate menu. It seemed easy on paper, (it always looks easy on paper). When it came time to shop and prep some things ahead, the kitchen was flooded with crates of herbs, baby vegetables and seaweed! I hired my friend, Charles, the Chef de Cuisine from the Four Seasons Hotel, to step in the day before the reception. He would continue my preparations and oversee the flow of the elaborate menu otherwise I would be '*In the Weeds*'. Thank goodness for Charles.

Julie's custom gown was designed with silk organza roses clinging to her slim shoulders, twining down to a tiny waist and exotic flowing bouffant skirt. Against her creamy complexion and dark curls, it was a perfect choice. She carried Calla lilies in a simple sheaf of greens wrapped with satin ribbons.

Paul, so handsome, was the perfect groom. Anton, father of the groom, looked gaunt, but seemed stable. I had been unsure if he would even turn up, as he was still under my restraining order since the tirade when he burned all my files. However, we had to put on a good face to the world for this important day.

After the formal service in the Catholic Church, the wedding party stopped at "The Yacht Club" for glamorous wedding photos out on their front lawn with the West Vancouver skyline across the water in the background. We all assembled for pictures. Once finished there, we headed over the Lions Gate Bridge to our hillside home for the big reception. A fresh oyster bar dressed with real seaweed and crushed ice, was set out on the front patio. Elegant hors d'oeuvres were passed to arriving guests while live music mellowed the scene. The afternoon sun broke through the clouds and lite-up the radiant faces of the newlyweds.

Many briny oysters and glasses of chardonnay later, we proceeded to a sit-down dinner in the living room and outdoor patios; tables draped with squares of white silk fabric accented with gold touches. The menu started with creamy lobster bisque; champagne chicken and comforting scalloped potatoes positioned with grilled vegetables was the entrée, and fresh garden greens followed to lighten the palate. In between the entree and the salad, grapefruit flavored granite was served. Of course the wedding cake was served last.

The cake, a spectacular genoise, fragrant with fresh flowers clinging to each layer, was ready for its entrance. Towering sponge cake tiers were filled with strawberries and crispy, kirsch-flavored meringue disks. The outside was finished with white chocolate butter cream/whipped cream, decorated with fresh, tiny bud gardenias, freesia and trailing ivy.

The cake was cut, petite, lemon tartlets were passed and we all drank champagne. It was the perfect wedding for the bride and groom. I was exhausted.

I kept up my energy until the last guest left, and then headed down to the bedroom alone, threw off my dress and shoes, to collapse into the covers with visions of the happy couple waving goodbye. I had pulled off one more stressful family event.

My few minutes of dreamland were abruptly brought to an end. Anton, still in the house, now really drunk, ripped off the quilts. With shouted obscenities, he pulled me out to the flood-lit kitchen to curse and ramble incoherently. He stumbled and crashed about the dirty dishes stacked in bus tubs on the floor. Tablecloths and spent floral décor were also piled in the messy kitchen, waiting for the morning clean-up. I was taken completely by surprise, incredulous, dumb-struck, after such a special day. None of the ambiance of the evening had rubbed off on him. I stood there, rubbing my eyes, unable to speak, unable to absorb such a tirade. I stood, my arms crossed in front, hugged myself and clung desperately to my nightgown.

Finally I said in a small voice, "This is the end, you're no longer my husband!" I was too tired to be afraid. Divorce was now definite for me.

The next day, I took the big leap, and started proceedings for divorce. I could not live this lie anymore.

Life continued to roll forward.

Anton's failure to take on any kind of work, and his erratic behavior was increasingly weird; he had not worked at any job for eight years. I knew he must have depleted all our stocks and savings after so many empty years. He used anything that could be turned into cash.

40

Words from a Psychic

On a whim, I joined my girlfriend to go to a psychic for a reading. I thought, "What could it hurt, maybe some good news." When she gave me a reading, without knowing anything about me, just my first name, she summed it up.

She turned on the tape recorder and I pressed my ring into her hand. "I see someone close to you, a male, it's very odd. It looks like he has just given up. He always earned a lot of money before, but for some reason he has just given up." She emphasized this several times. She gave me more things to ponder but her first words had hit it right on the head; he has just given up.

Years later as I dwell on the wedding fiasco again, I realize Anton saw Paul's wedding as one more victory for me and one more defeat for him. In his former position, he was always the leader. Now I had orchestrated the reception, I had created the food. It was my contact at the Four Seasons Hotel that Charles, the Chef de Cuisine was able to step in and carry on my menu in the kitchen the day before and day of the wedding.

Anton had become window dressing. He had let loose his anger, his self-pity in a drunken state, showing his inability to be in control. He had gone over the edge. I was speechless at his performance. He had saved all this frustration only for me.

WEDDING CAKE NO. 2

Paul and Julie's cake was a modern sponge base with almond butter cream and white chocolate finishing icing. The cake was tiered and had fresh flowers and ivy. The scent was like a heady woodland bouquet.

Medium
Yields one 11x15 rectangle and one 8x8 square and one 7" round.
Oven 350
Can be doubled.

Cake
¾ cup milk
6 Tbsp. unsalted butter
2⅓ cups <u>cake </u>flour
3 tsp. baking powder
1⅓ cups sugar
10 eggs
7 yolks, only
Orange zest
1 tsp. vanilla

Method
Cut parchment for bottom of selected pans. Spray bottom only, dust with flour, set aside.
Heat milk with butter, set aside but keep warm.
Over hot water, whisk eggs, yolks and sugar to dissolve sugar grains, (test with some between fingers).
Transfer mixture to large bowl and beat to triple volume.

Sift flour, baking powder. Quickly fold into egg mixture, adding milk last, down one side of bowl.
Fold up and over to keep egg mixture light.
Add zest/vanilla and pour into prepared pans.
Bake until lightly browned and surface springs back, about 15-20 minutes.
Cool in pans.
This is a nice moist sponge cake.

Almond Butter Cream
1⅓ cups sugar
1 cup water
12 egg yolks
2 lb. unsalted butter
1 tsp. almond extract

Method
Combine sugar/water in small, heavy sauce pan. Bring to boil without stirring.
Cover and let boil to dissolve sugar, 3-5 minutes.
Uncover and boil about 2 minutes to reach 238 on candy thermometer.
Meanwhile beat yolks until pale and light.
When syrup is ready, remove from heat, carefully pour down inside edge of mixing bowl in steady stream, beating on low.
Increase speed to high and beat until bowl is only just warm.
Add butter in small bits, add flavoring, beating as you go, until mixture comes together as smooth icing of piping consistency.
Extra can be frozen.

White Chocolate Butter Cream Icing
12 oz. good quality white chocolate
4 cups sugar
12 Tbsp. cornstarch
2 cups boiling water
¾ cup Crème de Cacao liqueur
3 lb. unsalted butter

Method
In a medium saucepan combine chopped chocolate, sugar and cornstarch.
Add boiling water, stir to combine and over medium heat stir until thickened.
Let cool briefly.
Add softened butter in small bits to slowly combine.
Whisk to correct piping texture. Add flavoring.
Refrigerate, covered and store <u>overnight, (this results in correct piping texture, bringing back from cold instead of trying to get it right from too hot).</u>

Final assembly of cakes
Choice of icing
Crème de Cacao liqueur
1flat of fresh raspberries
Apricot puree

For each layer use <u>two </u>cakes to get right height for wedding cake tiers.
Ponge, (soak), each cake surface with simple syrup and crème de Cacao.
Spread thin layer of apricot puree.

Add layer of Raspberries.
Do a crumb coat of outside icing.
Refrigerate until final decoration
Do for each tier.
Finish as for wedding cake using cake boards, and dowels for sturdiness.

41

Widowed

The forces of Ying and Yang are always at work. Without any warning my husband died on Good Friday, April of 1985, the victim of alcohol and a heart attack. He had been living in a rented apartment for the past three months in lower West Vancouver as a result of my restraining order. My boys found him, dead, in his business suit that Easter morning. They had come to wish him well on Easter. Minutes later, they were at my door with the sad news. I was a widow at fifty three. In searching my soul, I asked myself, "Could I have done anything more to prevent this outcome?" There was no answer.

How would I continue alone? I had no income from Anton. He had drained all our savings without my knowledge. Every credit card was useless. I discovered that I had no insurance, no investments and owed thousands of dollars in back taxes. The mortgage on our house was two years in arrears. At first I blocked out everything; "I cried, got mad, then I got angry. At night, alone in the darkened kitchen I sobbed until no more tears would come. I cursed him for leaving me, for dying, for all that had happened. How could he have done this?

What a coward, taking the easy way out of his predicaments." Now I truly had to look ahead.

With my house and kitchen in foreclosure and all my master files gone, I couldn't face trying to piece together a fresh school program for the 1986 winter/spring season. As long as I still had the house, it was necessary to keep up appearances. I didn't have time to be overwhelmed by it. Besides, The Bon Appétit photo shoot was scheduled for this summer, 1985. I had to concentrate on incoming catering supplying cash for the immediate future until I was forced out. Could I keep the bank and creditors at bay, at least until the magazine was in print? That would be another eight months.

My lawyer gave me some wise advice, He said, "No one would save me but me, so I'd better get on with it and figure it out. No white knight was going to suddenly appear."

I took my lawyer's advice, I hunkered down, looked forward not back. There were catering jobs ready to confirm and finances to be muddled through. Only a few of my friends and customers were aware of my husband's death, were aware of the sham of our marriage, were aware of the hideous state he had left me in. I had no time to dwell on the past, or think about the baggage I had to deal with. I had to keep my head up and somehow make lemonade out of lemons. It was business as usual.

During the next five months, large and small projects filled my days. A sit-down dinner at the Vancouver Aquarium for 150, pre-ballet hors d'oeuvres in the Vancouver Performing Arts Center for 300, an exciting presentation of Small Plates in the glittering showroom of the Porsche/Audi dealership launching a new product.

I was kept busy, on the best list for referrals, but I was still far from erasing the debt against our mortgage and back taxes.

Late at night I walked from room to room, whispered to the empty spaces, house, you were supposed to be my forever home, but you are going back to the bank for sure. Someone else will fill these rooms soon. Listen to their stories but do not forget me. Remember the laughter we once created here! I loved my renovated kitchen with my big Wolf stove, I loved the garden with the towering fir and cedar trees, loved the crystal blueness at the deep end of the swimming pool. After living here for almost thirty years it was so unfair to end this way. I had tried my best!" I wondered, what would become of me? I was allowing myself a moment of self-pity.

42
The Photo Shoot

All the planned catering jobs went by without a hitch. Each time an event was done and crossed off the books, I sighed and looked to the next extravaganza I had to create. My mind was on the up-coming Bon Appétit production. It had to be perfect. What great PR exposure. Maybe something wonderful would come from it.

The magazine shoot was spread over two days in August, a Sunday and Monday. An elaborate wedding for 150 was already on the books for the Saturday before.

My staff worked all night on Friday, completing the wedding buffet. I was using a corner counter alongside them finishing the four-tier wedding cake. A whole flat of perfect fresh, raspberries tumbled down over the cake layers clinging to the Kirsch butter cream. Clusters of romantic, full-blown, blush pink roses were the pièce de résistance added at the last minute. My fridges were bulging and ready for the set-up staff to slide everything out into the van for delivery.

I said, "I promised the Mother-of-the-Bride that I would personally be on site. I'll take the cake in the last load and oversee the banquet until all is underway." Joanne ran out into the garden to cut fresh greens for décor.

The Saturday wedding was done, now I could clear my mind toward the magazine photo shoot. This turn of events would crown me as the culinary queen of all things Croatian. I wondered if it galled Anton's mother that I, someone not even Croatian, was now the one to carry on the Miachika family recipes she held so dear, usurping her prestigious, matriarchal position. She had become instantly distant upon her son's untimely death. She would not accept his alcoholism: via the gossip grapevine, I was the cause of his death!

Sunday morning all the crew arrived; ten technicians, a food writer, a food stylist and a script director. Bon Appétit does everything in a professional manner. They brought in their gear, looked for electrical outlets, chattered among themselves and covered the floor with interconnecting cables, stands for the cameras and at last started to interact with me, my staged students, and my assistant, Joanne. The script had been carefully coordinated over many months ahead of time, between the technical crew and myself. We all knew where to begin. I said, "Just another day in the food business"

Joanne, my long time food friend and most trusted sous chef tried to calm me with, "Remember, this is no big deal, we've done stuff like this before." Such a rock, she always makes me laugh.

Miles of wiring, cameras and lights took over every spare inch in the kitchen. I held my breath and jumped in. First the pot roast and dumplings got underway. While they simmered in the top Thermador wall oven, I sautéed the fresh, delicate, pink speckled prawns, barely out of the salty Pacific Ocean, and fresh squid, (glutinous bodies and tentacles), for a marinated seafood presentation. Aunt Neda's Wedding Soup in a big stock pot on the stove-top was starting to tantalize everyone's noses with its fragrant goodness, chicken broth and petite veal meat balls. The meaty pork shanks and stuffed cabbage rolls topped with roasted garlic, created a fabulous earthy aroma. From that oven, wisps of flavor assaulted the senses, creating excitement in the kitchen. I worked steadily with intensity. Joanne touched my shoulder reminding me to look up and smile into the camera.

She was working on stuffing the yellow and red peppers so I could place them into a red enamel, lidded pot, going into my wide Wolf range at the end of the counter.

Years ago, when I was so fresh and eager to please, attired in little gingham dresses, I was so young, naïve and trusting. I momentarily allowed myself to slip back to the time when strudel and simple challenges had occupied my waking hours. So much had happened since then. Now I needed to push away the pain and hurt of the past, and prepare myself for my new life on my own. I forced the clinging cobwebs away.

Rinsing my hands I grabbed a fresh tea towel and looked over at the film crew and said, "I'm ready for the show stopper, the Apple Strudel." To myself I said, "Focus!"

The lights were blinding, the camera crew continued to give directions, "Turn your head, lean in closer to the table so we can get the whole effect. Students, look at the pastry, cluster closer to Barbara to create just the right effect."

With strudel dough clinging to my fingers I started to pull and stretch the dough over the patterned cloth that had been set out on a large round table. The pastry was now whisper thin. Apple slices, currants, lemon juice and zest, sugar and cinnamon were strewn over the dough with abandon. I spread finely chopped walnuts to the edges, next the whole pastry was rolled up like a jelly roll. It was brushed with melted butter and I placed it on a large sheet pa. It baked for about one hour. Strudel had been made so many times in this kitchen I knew it would turn out perfectly.

While I was busy cooking, the magazine's food writer was making notes, asking me questions and creating her story to print alongside the many pictures. It was so interesting to be part of something from the inside, to see it coming together. Over two days all the components of the planned menu materialized successfully and with the help of their food stylist it was finished. I wondered what it was all going to look like when the March issue came out on the news-stands. I would have nine months to wait.

Bon Appétit Magazine shows Barbara and students making Strudel

APPLE STRUDEL

Apple strudel is a big accomplishment. This is one of many recipes Bon Appétit included in their article on my cooking school. I had made strudel so many times, it was easy. Many of the current generation of Yugoslavs have not mastered this, leaving it for their mothers to continue the tradition.

Oven 425, 45 minutes
Difficult

Pastry
½ cup warm water
2 Tbsp. vegetable oil
1 Tbsp. sugar
2 cups all-purpose flour
1 egg
1 egg white
Extra vegetable oil

Filling
6-8 tart apples, Granny Smith type
2 Tbsp. fresh lemon juice
Melted butter (to brush surface of stretched dough)
½ cup currants
¼ cup sugar
¼ cup firmly packed brown sugar
Cinnamon
Freshly grated nutmeg
Grated lemon peel

½ cup toasted, chopped almonds
Buttered crumbs
Powdered sugar
Whipped cream optional

Method for pastry
Blend warm water, oil and sugar in small bowl to dissolve sugar.
Mound flour on counter. Next make a well in center. Add water mixture, egg and white to well.
Using one hand, with fingers, gradually draw in flour from edges until all flour is incorporated.
Gather into ball.
Slap over and over on counter about 100 times. This motion creates elasticity in the dough.
Rub dough with oil, set to rest in bowl, covered about 30 minute.

For filling
Peel, core apples, thinly slice, place in a bowl, sprinkle with sugar.

Assembly
Use a 48" round table covered with table cloth. Dust with flour. place dough in center.
Flatted dough into disc, press into large circle.
Remove any rings or jewelry that might cause a tear.
Begin stretching dough from underneath with rounded fingers and back of hands, pulling outward, and working around circle trying to not make holes.
Use coffee cups to hold edges from springing back.
When dough is hanging over edges, and is quite transparent, trim thick edges away. Discard this excess.

Brush surface with melted butter.

Scatter apple slices over dough to just one inch in from edges.

Sprinkle currants, sugar, grated nutmeg and cinnamon, over all parts of dough. Add zest and almonds.

Using table cloth as aid, roll up as for jelly roll, tucking in sides.

Lift onto greased or spayed sheet pan, curving to U shape to fit onto pan.

Brush with melted butter.

Bake at 425 for first 15 minutes.

Baste, then reduce heat to 350 and bake until golden brown, about 30 minutes.

Cool on pan, cut into 2' pieces, set out on serving plate.

Dust with icing sugar.

Add whipped cream in side dish, (optional).

<u>Chef note,</u> some people use buttered crumbs along edges of dough adding extra texture, sprinkling crumbs over surface as dough is rolled up.

BON APPÉTIT COOKING CLASS

aid of the tablecloth. She then moves it onto the baking sheet. "See how easy it is?" the teacher says with an encouraging smile to everyone.

Barbara believes the single most important step toward cooking well is being organized. "I tell my students they should have an 'order of battle,' with time slots for each step, for even the simplest meal. That way you don't panic because you know just how long it will take to get from A to Z, and you know you're not going to forget anything." She also feels it is a mistake to be too ambitious. "It's part of the fun to try out a new recipe or something very complicated on guests. That's fine. But then make all the other dishes easy things that you're familiar with. And read through every recipe,

even those you think you know by heart, before you start anything. It's amazing how often you find some key ingredient is missing from the cupboard or refrigerator ... especially if there are children around."

She begins most of her courses by advising students on the best sources in different parts of the city for ingredients, telling them how the individual items in a menu work together, and adding a few hints on wine appreciation. "Then I work through the menu, going over any tricky points. Finally, I show them how it's done, and encourage them to take notes and make drawings. I stress technique, but I try not to overwhelm people with too many difficult things. I plan the classes so both novice and experienced

WALNUT-RUM ROLLS

1 Lemon peel-studded dough is rolled out into two large rectangles.

2 Filling is made from ground walnuts, rum, sugar, butter and hot milk.

3 Dough is covered with filling, then rolled up and left for a final rising.

4 Brushed with egg glaze, walnut rolls emerge crusty and brown from the oven.

BON APPÉTIT·MARCH 1986 69

Bon Appétit Magazine photo shoot showing Walnut Rum Rolls production from start to finish.

43

His Highness the Aga Khan

More glamorous events came and went. A very special request was to produce and deliver dozens of decadent desserts for three days to a private home just up the hill from me here in the British Properties, in West Van. The person asking for all of this was a lady from one of my dessert classes. With her husband and children, she was a recent arrival from Iran. After each class, she passed all the cooking and baking information onto her cook to add to their Eastern cuisine.

She explained, "It is for a special guest coming to our home, namely, "The current Aga Khan." Wow! This is incredible. The only other royal person with this name I had ever heard of was the Aga Khan, from two decades ago, (the grandfather of this present Khan). In those days long ago, the Khan on his birthday was ceremonially weighed, in precious stones. It was all very outrageous because he was about 300 pounds. It was a show of great wealth.

Images of Bagdad and flying carpets swept into my imagination. Not very many people knew about Iran in 1985. I certainly didn't.

I was asked to provide pastries of all descriptions each day before tea time and also before breakfast if possible? Previous to being assigned this mission, The RCMP, (The Royal Canadian Mounted Police), did a background check of my suitability and non-subversive activities.

This was all going on in our residential neighborhood on the slopes of West Vancouver. The street approach had a van and several cars positioned on the curved driveway to prevent any direct access by uninvited guests. This was all very Mission Impossible!

I passed the police check; arranged my schedule to allow for such an arduous undertaking. I still had classes and other catering, but I was oozing energy and optimism.

Chocolate in every form made up many of the creations, because I was told it was his favorite flavor. Crisp pastries with milk chocolate layers and my Imperiale Cake, flourless, with dense, smouldering dark chocolate in every fork-full were two selections. A delicate white chocolate torte; a cake plus white chocolate mousse both flavored with Kirsch enrobing all in white chocolate buttercream icing, sprinkled with toasted pistachios, was created just for this occasion.

Petite tarts filled with fresh, lush raspberries. Caramelized almonds sprinkled over a delicate tea/orange flavored chiffon cake roll were soon devoured. All these sweets were laid out on the dining room table, like a gem filled carpet under a dazzling light from the iridescent blinding brightness of their opulent crystal chandelier.

The white chocolate torte was so different that His Highness asked if he could have a second cake, a duplicate, ready for eleven AM the next morning. His agenda was set for an early departure in his private jet back to Sardinia, Italy. Of course I made a second cake and carefully packaged it in my impressive blue box, with gold lettering and gold seal.

As he was leaving with his entourage around him, he spoke to me personally. "Thank you so much for your delightful pastries, plus this extra cake for my flight home," He presented me with a gold watch, a nice surprise. I felt like I had won an Oscar! When I teach that cake in class, I call it "His Highness Gateau." recounting the above story and name dropping just a little.

HIS HIGHNESS GATEAU

This special cake was one of my inventions for His Highness the Aga Khan when he visited Vancouver and I was asked to supply pastries for him for breakfast and tea time. A little nervous about the whole thing, I pulled out all the stops and created this white chocolate, rectangular layer cake. You must use only real, not coating 'White Chocolate'.

Serves 10
Oven 350
Middle rack
Sheet pan
Medium

8 oz. white chocolate, chopped
½ cup unsalted butter, room temperature
1 cup sugar
8 eggs, separated
¼ cup crème de Cacao
1 cup ground almonds (Blend both cookies and almonds together)
1 cup Amaretto cookies, ground

Method
Prepare sheet pan with parchment. Set aside.
Melt chocolate over hot, not boiling water set aside.
In medium bowl, beat butter, sugar and egg yolks until light and well blended.
Add melted chocolate and liqueur.
Fold in almonds and cookies.

Beat whites with pinch of salt, stiff but not dry.
Fold whites into batter in three stages.
Pour batter onto parchment lined sheet pan.
Bake 20 minutes or until cake tester comes away clean, and light finger imprint springs back. Cool, leave on parchment.

Butter Cream Filling

8 oz. white chocolate, chopped and melted
¾ cup sugar
3Tbsp. cornstarch
½ cup boiling water
¼ cup Crème de Cacao
¾ lb. unsalted butter, room temperature

Method

Combine in saucepan white chocolate with sugar and cornstarch.
Mix, then add boiling water and stir over medium heat until thickened.
Let cool, then stir in flavorings.
Beat butter in mixer bowl. Add cooled, thickened chocolate mixture.
Beat until smooth and glossy, of piping texture.

Assembly

Cut cake into three cross sections. Place on cake board to fit.
Fill layers with butter cream. Spread butter cream over top and sides.
Pipe a decorative criss-cross pattern over top.
Optional finish, add sugared sliced almonds on sides. (see index for recipe)

CRYSTALLIZED GINGER SABLES, ENGLISH SHORTBREAD COOKIES

Here are perfect shortbread cookies to have in the pantry. These could be a special addition for His Highness's morning cup of coffee.

Oven 350
Bottom ⅓ rack in oven
Makes 24
Easy

2cups flour
⅔ cup plus 2Tbsp. sugar
¾ cup plus 2 Tbsp. unsalted butter, soft
1 egg
Crystallized ginger, finely chopped

<u>Method</u>
Combine flour and ⅔ cup sugar until well blended.
Mix in butter with fingers or use short pulses with processor.
Add egg and knead just until combined.
Shape into a log about 2" in diameter.
On parchment, sprinkle remaining 2 tb sugar and ginger pieces, using paper to aid pressing onto surface of log.
Roll log in plastic and refrigerate for at least 1 hour.
Preheat oven to 350.

Unwrap log, slice into ⅓' coins. Place 1" apart on greased cookie sheet.
Bake 12-15 minutes until golden.
Transfer to rack.
Store in an air tight container.

PRUNE ICE CREAM

Prunes are used in a lot of French recipes but are often over looked here in America. This is an unusual combination to use with purchased Vanilla Ice cream. Guests can hardly ever guess the flavor. Have this in your freezer for unexpected company.
Very unusual combination of ingredients. This is a beautiful and simple ice cream. His Highness loved it.

10 dried, but soft prunes
Armagnac liqueur
Rich Vanilla ice cream
Easy

Method
Soak prunes in liqueur warming slightly, then chop to medium size pieces.
Puree 2-3 pieces of prunes.
Soften ice cream, fold in prunes and carefully swirl in puree, don't over mix or the ice cream will look muddy.
Re-pack in container. Freeze.

44

House for Rent

I had to make money! I was still in my house but knew it was only two months before I would have to move out. But to where? Everything was so uncertain.

From January through October, Vancouver was hosting Expo '86. The city was expecting a flood of tourists. The Chamber of Commerce was encouraging residents to register their private homes for short-term rental listing the type of accommodations and number of rooms and special perks. I had never considered such a thing, but I had this big house and a glamorous pool. Anton had died in March, the winter before and I was desperate for money to survive at least until the Bon Appétit Magazine was on the street. I hoped something good would come from it. My future was so uncertain.

My girlfriend Margo said, "Why don't you give it a try? The money would be a help, besides it could be fun and everyone is supposed to be pre-screened for safety."

I thought about it and promptly listed my house.

West Vancouver Home
Three Bedrooms, Gourmet Kitchen
Glamorous Pool,
Grand Landscaping
Capilano Golf and Country Club, across the street

A group of six Native American Indians from Winnipeg, Alberta booked my house for a three-day weekend. They were coming to town for a tribal meeting with the Capilano Tribe close by in North Vancouver, not for Expo at all. Whatever, it would be quick money and sounded okay. Arrival was scheduled for 4 PM Friday afternoon. I was away from the house for an errand and planned to return in plenty of time to greet my guests. As I turned into my driveway I could see an unfamiliar car parked in front of my garage.

Quelle suprise! My front door was ajar. How could that happen? I had locked it before leaving at two PM. I was nervous. As I approached the front door, I could hear raucous laughter and noises of obvious drinking, beer cans clunking. I crept in and followed the noise into my kitchen amazed to see six burly men sitting at my kitchen table, obviously enjoying their surroundings with a table of now empty beer cans.

"What are you doing? How did you get in?" I was so astounded, incredulous, sort of gasping for breath. A break-in; burglars, did they have guns? No, these must be my weekend guests!

One guy said "Oh, yeah, I just crawled in through your kitchen window, and by the way the pool is so warm, we had a swim already." He made it sound so normal, breaking into someone's house. I know ethics on the Reservation are different. They have their own laws. I didn't feel too safe. I surveyed my dilemma, looked at these six big men, and pretended I was in control.

I tried to take it all in stride, gave them a key, laid down a few rules and went over the bedroom layout. I said," 'If you use the pool again, leave all your wet towels in the basket, and I will put them in the laundry. I have lots more dry towels and will leave them out for you." What had I let myself in for?

Then I said, "I will have juice, coffee, scrambled eggs and bacon for your breakfast, ready at seven in the morning." With that they retired to the bedroom wing and I had the kitchen, the loft with a guest bed and the rest of the house to myself. I reminded myself, it was cash up front, four-hundred- fifty dollars for three days. The next morning at six-o'clock, the house was engulfed with the floating fingers of aroma from crisp puff pastry apple tarts just coming out of the oven. All was well. My 'Natives' turned out to be perfect guests.

Over that spring during Expo 86, I had more renters. One time it was the executive director of the San Francisco Ballet and her family. They seemed to really like the idea of the pool and the golf course just half a block away. Her husband had reciprocal rights from his golf club in San Francisco so getting a tee time at the prestigious Capilano Golf and Country Club, wasn't difficult.

I worked all these bookings in and around my scheduled food projects and weddings. The unexpected money, about eleven thousand dollars, really helped. The income from my many catering jobs continued to flow, but it wasn't enough to assuage my mortgage problem but I think all this gave me the impetus to go forward.

APPLE YOGURT BREAKFAST TARTS

These delicious tarts were a big hit with my beer drinking guests. They paid the bill in cash, up front and three days later the house was empty again. These following recipes work well for quick preparation.

Oven 425
Serves 12
3" flan tart tins, removable bottom

Filling
6 Granny Smith apples, cored, peeled, quartered, then sliced thin
1 8oz. plain yogurt
4 Tbsp. honey
2 Tbsp. chopped walnuts
2 eggs
Pinch salt
½ cup sugar
Vanilla

Use apricot puree for glazing after baking.

Pastry
4½ cups flour
3Tbsp. Sugar
3 tsp. salt
1½ cups cold, unsalted butter, diced
9 Tbsp. orange juice
3 tsp. vanilla

Method

Place flour, salt sugar in processor. Pulse on/off.

Add cold butter, pulse quickly.

Add orange juice and vanilla. Pulse just to crumbly stage.

Turn out onto plastic, press together. Press into disc.

Roll out pastry to ⅛ thickness, drape over tins, press to fit, trim edges.

Fan apple slices across each tart. Next, spoon the filling over apples.

Bake 425 for 45 minutes until well browned.

Brush with glaze while still warm.

BLUEBERRY-LEMON CRISP

Oven 350, 35 minutes then 15 more
Serves 6

4 cups fresh blueberries
1 tsp. instant tapioca
4 tsp. sugar
1 tsp. lemon zest
1 tsp. almond extract

Topping
4 cups fresh bread crumbs
5 Tbsp. cold butter
½ cup brown sugar

3 Tbsp. sliced almonds

Method
Toss blueberries with tapioca, lemon zest, sugar and extract.
Place in baking dish.
In a separate bowl, mix crumbs, brown sugar and butter with
fingers to crumbly stage.
Resist the urge to add additional, different berries to mix as it
is wonderful just as it is.
Bake about 35 minutes, remove and add sliced almonds,
return to oven for 15 minutes more.
Serve warm with ice cream or just as is.
Wash additional berries and freeze for off season baking.

APPLE/CRANBERRY CRISP

Fresh cranberries are used when in season, but frozen berries work just as well. This dessert is welcome at the end of a rich meal or wonderful addition for an autumn buffet table. My mind was still in the catering mode.

12 servings
Oven 350, 1 hour
10x16 baker dish

Filling
12 Granny Smith apples, peeled, cored and sliced
8 oz. cranberries
Juice of 1 lemon
⅓ cup brandy
⅓ cup sugar
1 tsp cinnamon
2 Tbsp. whole wheat pastry flour

Topping
1½ cup regular rolled oats
½ cup toasted wheat germ
1 tsp. sea salt
1½ tsp. cinnamon
½ cup brown sugar, packed
⅓ cup canola oil
⅓ cup maple syrup

Method

Toss apples with cranberries, lemon juice, brandy, sugar, cinnamon and flour.

Place in bottom of dish.

Mix rolled oats, wheat germ, salt, cinnamon, brown sugar, oil and syrup.

Spread over apples, cover dish with foil. Bake 20 minutes. Uncover and bake 40 minutes longer, until apples are soft. Serve plain or with frozen vanilla yogurt type ice cream.

45
More 'Just Desserts'

BOSTON CREAM PIE

This classic recipe is so plain but be careful to give it just the right amount of pastry cream and chocolate Ganache finish. I made it several times before I got it just right. The pastry cream needs to be thick enough but not stiff. There are a lot of instructions for such a simple cake, but follow all and you will be pleased. (Look to the front book cover for a slice of this delicate cake). Here is the final set of ingredients for you.

8-9" cake pans, greased and bottoms covered with parchment.
Preheat oven 350. Bake about 20 minutes.
Medium

Cake
½ cup cake flour
¼ cup all-purpose flour
1 tsp. baking powder
¼ tsp salt
2 Tbsp. milk
4 Tbsp. unsalted butter
½ tsp. vanilla
5 eggs, room temperature
¾ cup granulated sugar
¼ tsp. cream of tartar

Method
Use the lower middle rack for cake pans.
Whisk flours, baking powder and salt together.
Heat milk and butter in a small saucepan, keep warm.
Add vanilla.
Separate eggs, placing whites in a standing mixer, reserve yolks in a small bowl.
Beat whites at high speed until foamy. Gradually add 6 Tbsp. of sugar and cream of tartar to beat to soft moist peaks.
Put meringue in a large stainless bowl.
Use the same mixer bowl to whisk the yolks adding the last 6 Tbsp. of sugar at high speed until it is pale and thick.
Add the meringue to the yolks in the mixer bowl, but do not mix yet.
Sprinkle the flours over the whites and yolks and on low speed mix for 10 seconds.
Remove the mixer bowl and by hand pour the melted butter down the side of the bowl.

With a spatula fold mixture gently but quickly only until
no trace of whites and flour. Make sure the butter is also
absorbed into all.

Immediately pour batter into 2 pans. Bake until cake tops are
light brown and spring back when touched.
Cool on a rack. Remove parchment paper.
Ponge surfaces of cake with rum syrup, (½ cup water, ½ cup
sugar, 2 Tbsp. rum. Heat gently to combine.

Pastry Cream
1 Tbsp. butter
2 cups whole milk
2 cups heavy cream
4½ Tbsp. cornstarch
5 eggs
1 tsp. vanilla
½ cup sugar

Method
Bring milk/cream to a boiling point in a medium sauce pan.
Combine sugar, cornstarch and eggs in a mixer bowl and
whip to form ribbons.
Slowly add hot milk to egg mixture, whisking. Put all back into
saucepan and boil for 1 minute to thicken.
Transfer and strain into a clean bowl. Add vanilla. Cover
surface with plastic wrap and chill preferably overnight.
Ponge surfaces of cake with rum syrup, then fill center of
cake with pastry cream, piling higher in middle then top with
second cake pressing lightly to force cream to edges. This will
give a really generous, impressive filling. Chilling cake now
allows the pastry cream to settle before finishing and cutting.

Chocolate Ganache Glaze
6 oz. chocolate, chopped
½ cup heavy cream
1 Tbsp. light corn syrup

Method
Bring cream to a boil, pour over chocolate to melt. Let sit 3 minutes then add corn syrup and stir lightly to combine. Use when still slightly warm but quite thick, to pour over cake. Let it drizzle down the sides

Additional idea. You can use sugared, sliced almonds pressed to cake sides.

46
A New Direction

It was March 1986. The Bon Appétit Magazine was on the news-
stands. When I saw the ten pages of pictures and flowing story
alongside, all I could say was, "Wow," I experienced a real flash of
fame.

The article entitled, "The Robust Cuisine of Yugoslavia," generated
more exposure than I could ever have imagined. The phone started
ringing off the hook. I answered, "Cuisine de Barbara Cooking
School," and most questions were the same.

"Tell me about your school. When will your next series be? Can
you send information to me, right away? When was the last time you
were in Yugoslavia? Is it fabulous there?" But one voice was different.

"Hello, I'm Stewart Ritchie 111, MD, owner of Guckenheimer
Food Contract Services, a boutique food service company in San
Francisco. I have your impressive Bon Appétit article in my hand,
and wonder if you would consider joining our family business as
our corporate chef and food specialist? We are not quite like your
glamorous school, but I think you will be excited at the scope and
challenge waiting for you. We operate contract cafeterias in corporate

buildings. Betty, a friend of yours, and ours, speaks so highly of your talents; with food, décor, and your presentation and teaching skills." Right there on the phone it was agreed that he would arrange a flight and accommodations for a three-day visit to the San Francisco area and Redwood City where the his corporate office was situated. Such a blur of excitement! I was flabbergasted by his offer!

I thought back to my midnight meeting with Betty the Christmas before, and our wistful projections of what might be? Was this going to be my next step?

Betty, my long-time friend from grade school was back in Vancouver to visit her family during the Christmas holidays. Was it a coincidence that our lives came together again at this time? We reminisced on the phone about Anton's death the previous spring, and about the magazine article that would be in print in three months. She was very thrilled for me and wishful it would thrust me into a good space.

Betty had lived and worked in San Francisco for many years, so she planted the seed that I should move to the city of food and culture to take advantage of my turn of good fortune. She said, "You've worked so hard for your credits, your children are almost all on their own, you're a new widow, now is your time!" Let this knowledge carry you through to the next edge.

We arranged to meet at her mother's house on New Year's Eve after I had delivered a late night buffet of caviar on ice, cracked crab and profiteroles dipped in crunchy caramel for a soiree at the glamorous Kaiser family apartment in downtown Vancouver.

Talking into the early morning hours, we were like school girls again. She said, "Of course you must stay at my place in the Marina in San Francisco while you look for your own flat and career possibilities. I will help you find your way. I know the city really well."

Who knew what the magazine article would produce. Everything was up in the air…I was open to ideas. When Dr. Ritchie called that

March, my path was put into motion. I was going to survive for now! All the planets and stars in my horoscope must have been aligned and in my favor! I continued to believe in Angels.

The excursion to San Francisco was custom made for me. It all looked better than I could have imagined. Someone was going to pay me a salary, with health benefits. I was at the right place at the right time. The position was described as high powered food merchandising melded with chef training and menu development.

My passion for food was my saving talent and without knowing it, I had been preparing myself for this position all my life. I said to myself, "You can do it, this is just like running your school but on a bigger scale."

My house was sold and I would have to be out by the end of August. I still had several catering contracts on the books and one more wedding. David and Sharon planned to marry in July.

I wondered about this closing chapter of my first life: Will I be good enough to survive in San Francisco?

The new job in San Francisco meant taking a big risk; changing countries, leaving my aging mother, my sons and daughters-in-law, my friends, and giving away my two trusty German-Shepherd dogs. I weighed the odds, I had to do it. Even though I would be out of sight, would my family hold my image close? I whispered, "Keep me in your heart."

BON APPETIT COOKING CLASS

The Robust Cuisine of Yugoslavia

An Energetic Teacher in Vancouver Translates Heritage Specialties for the Modern Kitchen

BY JUNE R. GADER

BARBARA MIACHIKA is a pixieish blond with outrageous supplies of energy and stamina, an organizational bent that could send shivers through any corporate superstructure, and an inventiveness that finds its outlet in teaching, catering and other ventures involving her great love: food.

In serene, green Vancouver, where interest in international cooking and dining is just now approaching mania, Barbara has developed a loyal and ever-growing following for the ambitious classes she has been teaching for nine years. "I've never seen anyone give so much information in a single class," says one student who has taken several courses from her. "She gives you everything from a complete menu to techniques and tips, plus how to select the appropriate wines." That enthusiasm is echoed by the other participants gathered for today's special course in Yugoslavian cooking.

Barbara explains her fascination with this unusual cuisine as she prepares ingredients for the demonstration. "My late husband was born in Yugoslavia, though his family moved here when he was a baby," she says. "I fell in love with my mother-in-law's cooking, so she taught me all the recipes that had been handed down from generation to generation. Then my husband and I started visiting Yugoslavia on vacations, searching out relatives—there's one entire village on the coast that's peopled with Miachikas—and having fabulous meals. I decided the rest of the world needed to know how wonderful Yugoslavian food is."

Her kitchen was designed to communicate that message: An enormous

OPPOSITE: A showcase of superb ethnic fare (clockwise from top right)—pot roast with potato-semolina dumplings and red wine sauce; hearty cabbage rolls with pork hocks and roasted garlic; rice-stuffed peppers; cool Adriatic seafood salad; lamb patties in a rich Cognac-peppercorn sauce; traditional bread sticks; and Dalmatian wedding soup. RIGHT: Barbara Miachika displays two delectable finales, apple strudel dusted with powdered sugar, and slices of golden walnut-rum rolls.

Opening picture for Bon Appétit Magazine showing Barbara with her baked delicacies and certificates featured in the March 1986 article.

47

Still Catering

RASPBERRY MERINGUES WITH CHANTILLY CREAM

These next two recipes are part of my catering repertoire. The first is a simple but effective dessert. It travels well. The ice cream on the next page is also yummy! In France, village boulangeries sell ready made clouds of dry meringue to use like the following recipe.

Serves 10
Pre-heat oven 250, very low. Have a temperature gauge on rack in oven for accuracy.
Easy

9 egg whites
15 oz. icing sugar, sifted

1 ½ lb. fresh raspberries makes 1½ cups raspberry sauce. (½ cup water, 1 tb sugar, plus raspberries), bring to a boil, strain).

Chantilly Cream
1 Tbsp. sugar
1 tsp. vanilla
2 cups whipping cream

Method
Preheat oven to 250. Grease/flour sheet pan.
Whisk whites adding ½ of icing sugar, beating to stiff, glossy peaks.
Fold in last of sugar.
Shape with large serving spoon to create mounds of meringue.
Sprinkle lightly with extra icing sugar just before baking.
Bake until dry and pale. 1¾ hours.

Assembly
Whip cream adding sugar and vanilla. Spoon berries into bottom of serving bowl, (clear glass).
Layer some Chantilly cream over berries.
Crumble the dry meringue into large pieces.
Continue to layer. End with cream swirled for decoration.
Looks like English Trifle but no cake.
Serve with sauce.

LIME RUM ICE CREAM

Limes have such a wonderful flavor and aroma. Here in Florida limes right off my own tree are like perfume. Store bought are almost as good. Lime Rum Ice-cream is just right for a sophisticated finish to a dinner party. There are some inexpensive ice cream machines, but I happen to have a Simac Gelato Magnum from Italy, so I do make ice cream quite often.

Limes, about 10, wash, peel removed with vegetable peeler, then squeeze limes to make 1 ⅛ cups strained juice.
2 cups sugar
1 qt. half and half
1 Tbsp. light corn syrup
½ tsp. Kosher salt
2 Tbsp. Meyers rum

Method
Combine peel and sugar in processor with sharp blade and process until peel is very finely minced and sugar is almost liquid.
Add juice, pulse to combine, scrape into large mixing bowl.
Stir in half and half and salt. Add corn syrup.
Add rum. Be careful adding the rum as more than 2 Tbsp. might impinge freezing.

Strain out peel, then freeze according to manufacturer's instructions.

<u>**Note**</u>, stays zippy 4-5 days.
Press plastic over ice cream on top to prevent crystals.

48
David and Sharon's Wedding

In spite of no contact or support from Anton's side of the family, I felt strong and happy arranging this last wedding. I would hold both roles, Mother and Father, to send David and Sharon off to their new world. How could I give them the grand start they deserved? Using our house for the reception was not possible as it would soon belong to someone else. All our fancy club memberships had been rebuked. It was a conundrum. Problems often produce results and this is what emerged.

Paul said, "I'm still a junior member at Royal Van...like, how about that?" So it was decided to hold the reception there, at the Yacht Club. I would make the cake; it would be the last one for now!

Sharon chose a flattering wide brimmed hat of chiffon and lace to compliment her off shoulder bouffant gown. She looked so wonderful in a hat. The four bridesmaids at first couldn't agree on the dresses for themselves, and asked, "Can you suggest/or make the dresses for us?" I was honored by their confidence.

Always the mother of the groom, it was so special to be included in the bridal arrangements.

I found a perfect fabric in a soft shade of peach. Delicate silk chiffon can be tricky to work with but I felt no fear and proceeded with trust in my own ability. At my peak of energy I cut out all four dresses, working into the night, adjusting the main pattern for each girl. When all the gowns fitted perfectly I allowed myself a sigh of relief. They looked dreamy.

The girls were so pleased. They said in unison, "Thank you." Sharon was thrilled when she saw the girls in their finished gowns.

The result of our efforts as a family was a tribute to us all that no problem was too big. My one big thorn; I felt obliged to invite Anton's side of the family, even though they had disowned me, and had not spoken to me since Anton's death. They were my kids grandparents, so for children's sake, the invitations went out to them. Maybe they wouldn't come, but they did. I regretted that later. I didn't know what to expect from the Miachika side of the family. Now I had to save time to create their wedding cake and plan my own dress.

The Yacht Club was a classic setting, a cloudless day, with the sun glinting off the boats at dock, their hulls rocking gently in the waves, all the multi-colored flags appearing to wave good luck. The Bride and Groom with their entourage presented a once in a lifetime photo. The moment hangs indelibly in my memory. It was a sit down dinner for ninety. The gay laughter of the Wedding Party floated across the room like a warm blanket enclosing us in its soft folds. Sharon and David's wedding cake stood proudly on the head table for all extended family and friends to see; the sensual aroma of butter cream mingled with freesia and real roses. The scent of fresh raspberries... five towering tiers of delicate genoise ponged with Kirsch syrup, filled with white chocolate mousse, and the raspberries, those plump juicy berries, clinging to top and sides among the flowers as if thrown on with abandon, this was my crowning effort for the newly- weds. This cake was quite a bit like Paul and Julie's cake but with subtle changes, different flowers and slightly different finishing decoration with the raspberries.

As for the Miachika's they were very much in their own clique at the reception so I tried to ignore the fact of past hurt and present rudeness. I didn't have time to worry about them. I just held my breath and concentrated on the other guests.

MANGO MOUSSE RING

This smooth, tantalizing, molded mixture can be a buffet main course salad or a delightful dessert by just adding fresh berries into the center of the ring. It was a perfect addition to David and Sharon's wedding menu. I have a friend who calls me long distance just to renew the directions for this creation each time she makes it.
Easy

3 large packages of lemon Jell-O
4 cups boiling water
1 jar mango slices, drained, pureed, saving the liquid
2-8 oz. packages cream cheese, room temperature

Method

Dissolve Jell-O in boiling water. Add mango juice, pureed mango and cream cheese.
Spin in processor in two batches to create a smooth mixture.
Brush metal or glass mold with almond flavored oil; then pour mixture into mold. Allow to firm up in refrigerator 6 hours or overnight.
Turn out on rimmed platter, fill center with fresh blackberries or raspberries.

BISCOTTI

Biscotti are those ethnic biscuits that have now caught on with the latte and espresso crowd. I was introduced to the original European version from my Mother-in-law so many years ago. She called these Hungarian Toasts, so funny because she was Yugoslavian. These were her standby treat, always her special cookie, and she always made them the same way, with anise flavoring. At first it was a strange flavor, (licorice), but soon I liked it. Many years have gone by and all kinds of additions have surfaced; crystallized ginger, chocolate, and cranberries are some. This was Mrs. Sr.'s token unexpected surprise contribution to David and Sharon's wedding.

Oven 350,
30 minutes, remove from oven, turn to other side, to bake 15 minutes more. This makes them completely dry and crisp.
Easy

1 cup vegetable oil
1 cup sugar
2 cups all-purpose flour
2 cups cake flour
4 eggs
1 cup toasted, ground almonds, fine
1 cup unsweetened coconut
2 tsp. baking powder
½ tsp. salt
1 tsp. almond extract
1 Tbsp. anise extract

Method

Beat oil, eggs, sugar and extracts.

Add almonds and coconut to mixture.

Sift flours, baking powder and salt, adding to the bowl.

Knead on floured counter; shape into two long logs rounding off tops.

Place on greased sheet pans.

Bake in middle oven for 30 minutes.

Remove and when cool enough to handle but still hot, remove to cutting board and slice into ⅓ " slices on diagonal.

Place cut side up, return to oven for 15 minutes.

Turn slices over to dry other side. Return to oven for 15 minutes more.

Cool on rack.

Store Biscotti in an air tight container. They keep very well.

BARBARA'S VERSION

My own modern version of Biscotti has changing flavors and keeps evolving to suit the event.

Here is my current variation using corn meal, hazel nuts and pistachios. No oil.
Oven 325, 30-40 minutes, then cut, place pieces on sheet pan cut side up, and return to oven and bake 15 minutes, turn, bake 15 minutes more. Cool on wire rack. Store cookies in an air tight container.
Easy

2½ cups all-purpose flour
1 cup yellow cornmeal
¾ cup brown sugar
1½ Tbsp. lemon zest
1 Tbsp. orange zest
2 tsp. baking powder
½ tsp. kosher salt
2 large eggs
½ cup water
1 tsp. vanilla
¼ cup orange marmalade
1¼ cups toasted whole, shelled hazelnuts
½ cup golden raisins

<u>Method</u>
Spray 2-11x17 sheet pans.
Whisk flour, cornmeal, baking powder, brown sugar, zests and salt together.

In medium bowl whisk eggs, add water, vanilla and marmalade.

Stir wet ingredients into dry, mixture might be sticky. Mix in raisins and whole nuts.

Total 1 hour, 10 minutes. Yield 5 dozen.

Flour counter, turn out dough, knead and mix by hand shaping into 2 logs about 17" long.

Set logs on one sheet pan, pressing lightly to flatten top.

Bake 40 minutes in middle of oven. Don't over-bake at this point.

Remove to rack to cool only until able to handle.

Holding log at a slight angle, cut into ⅓" slices.

Place pieces flat on sheet pan, bake 15 minutes, remove, turn, bake 15 minutes more. Cool, store in container with tight lid.

Serve with coffee or hors d'oeuvres.

My Second Life

49

Guckenheimer

Lots of hugs, tears, good luck and good-byes filled me with excitement, but I still felt apprehensive. Would I be good enough to carry it off? Guckenheimer described me as "The Julia Child of Canada," a bit over the top. I have to remember Julia was self- taught at first too. Again, my silent prayer to my children; don't forget me, worry for me, keep me in your prayers.

The car trip to San Francisco loomed ahead. Paul said, "I'll take a few days from work and drive with you to make sure you don't get lost. I know the city pretty well from all my sailing/regatta visits there. The St. Francis Yacht Club is right in the place called the Marina, the same area as Betty's flat. I want you to reach her place okay. We don't want to worry." I accepted his concern gratefully. So it was decided.

A few pieces of luggage, my folders of recipes, a TV, some clothes, and my tennis racquet filled the back of my mini-van. It was all so weird. The rest of my household; furniture, kitchen supplies, décor, and clothes would have to stay behind in a storage locker until I had a new address, a visa, or a green card.

Betty greeted me with open arms and so the transition was made. Paul returned to Vancouver on the next available plane and it was done. I was on my own.

Betty's flat was in an old but desirable building in the fashionable Marina area. Because she had lived there for eleven years, the rent was grandfathered in, so low it would have been silly for her to even think of moving elsewhere.

We immediately started to plan the next moves for my survival. Over tea, Betty said, "Scour today's rent adds and I will tell you if the area is safe."

"How about this one," I said, "It sounds sensible and reads like it might be all right for now. Listen"…and I read the few lines of description;

Classic mansion, single rooms,
Rent, full board, day, week, and month.
Pacific Heights.

Betty said, "That is just up the block, it could work out. It's a recent listing. You must go tomorrow to check it out, while you can view it all in daylight, before the best rooms are taken." She was so optimistic.

Betty went off to work the next morning, and I set out to find a possible new home just up the hill. The building was an impressive mansion, in its hey-day, an aristocratic Pink Palace for one family. The immense front entry consisted of antique mirrored walls, a huge oriental carpet, and a Hollywood swirling staircase to the upper floors. A warren of rooms divided the inside of this glamorous shell into a boarding house atmosphere, allowing an up-scale address at a reasonable price for a short stay in this famous city. Professional men and women, mostly mid-thirties created a lively bunch. Breakfast and dinner was included. This was so much better than a hotel but still not a home.

I said, "I'll take it." to the concierge/manager when he showed
me the only vacancy. It wasn't much to look at, one room, a single
bed, a closet, and a bathroom with only a shower, no bathtub. I was
unhappy about no tub. I reasoned with myself it was only temporary
until I was sure about the job and all arrangements.

As I walked back down the hill I was overcome with doubts.
From years of security in a glamorous home to a single room with no
bathtub, such uncertain times ahead made it seem all so crazy.

When Betty returned from work that day, she could see I was
depressed and scared showing my true feelings for the first time.

She said, "Leave the past behind, just keep looking ahead. You
can do it; you made a go of the cooking school, you impressed Dr.
Ritchie, you're stronger and smarter than you think. You can succeed
on your own." She was a steady friend.

She said, "You can practice your first assignment in my kitchen,
to get the juices flowing" (a luncheon for forty Charles Schwab share-
holders at his downtown corporate office.) "That way I get to eat your
scrumptious cooking and afterward you can soak in my deep bathtub
filled with bubbles and hot water up to your neck. I'll even set out my
English scented soaps. Don't worry about the dishes, I'll clean up,"
It was a fun and relaxed start, allowing me to do what I loved while
working out the jitters.

Charles Schwab was one of several hundred contracts of
Guckenheimer Contract Food Service. Chuck was a personal friend
of Dr. Ritchie. I was obviously on show!
My first carefully chosen menu was as follows;

Cream of Carrot Soup, Crème Fraîche Swirl
Crusty Baguettes
Poached North Coast Salmon Medallions with a
Chinese, Candied Ginger Glaze
Citrus Beurre Blanc

Asparagus Spears, Sautéed Potato Ovals
Frittered Zucchini Flowers
Zabaglione Topped with Fresh Berries
Sablé Biscuits

The food service kitchen was well equipped with gas fired stoves and hot boxes for catered events. The Schwab kitchen manager placed my produce and fish order and I shopped in Chinatown for some of the unusual stuff myself.

The daily breakfast and lunch production for the cafeteria worked around my cutting board as I plunged into my menu. I was given one prep helper from the kitchen staff to aid me in managing food for forty people. Everything went smoothly. Just as I had planned, the courses came together. Tuxedoed staff arrived to whisk it all up to the twenty-third floor for presentation and table service. Of course it was a huge success, my trepidation was for naught, and I was on my way.

SPA CARROT/BUTTERNUT SQUASH SOUP FOR CHUCK

A fragrant and smooth butternut and carrot soup was my starter for the Charles Schwab luncheon. Perfect for catering and healthy, just the image Mr. Schwab wanted.

Serves 20 do x 2 for 40

3 large onions
2 tsp. cumin, thyme ground coriander
2 bunches fresh cilantro, minced
3 lb. carrots, peeled, chopped
3 Butternut squash, peeled, ½"cubed
2 large potatoes, peeled, diced
½ head celery, chopped
1½ gal chicken stock (each gal is 16 cups)

<u>Method</u>
Sauté onions in vegetable oil to wilt and brown them lightly.
Add vegetables, add herbs to blend flavors.
Add stock and water to cover if needed.
Bring to boil, simmer so squash is soft.
Take ½ mixture and puree in food processor in batches.
Taste for seasonings.
Add cilantro for garnish.
Optional. (Crème fraîche to swirl on top of each serving bowl).

The corporate office of the boutique Guckenheimer Food Service Company was located in Redwood City, about thirty minutes south of San Francisco. I was soon familiar with the corporate staff, their duties, and sort of comfortable with my own job description, Food Marketing Specialist and Corporate Chef. Dr. Ritchie had created this new job description just for me, hiring from the outside, not from within.

A lot was expected of me and not everyone was friendly. I had assumed they would love me and my new ideas. Ha! Ha! After all, Dr. Ritchie, the owner and president had hired me himself. I had felt so secure but this produced some jealousies and mutterings which I soon heard via the grapevine. Corporate life was trickier than I thought. When introduced to the existing managers at these cafeteria style food facilities it was important to go slowly and not step on toes. Some saw me as possibly threatening their world, their routine, their job. This was so much more than just Cooking! It was a whole learning experience for me, to be patient, to smooze, to be part of a big operation. Welcome to the multi layers of a corporate world!

A male associate within the company, my Champion, counseled me, "People have to get comfortable with you first, then be open to the new ideas you are trying to instigate. Don't rush into anything. The corporate world advances in tiny steps." I filed these bits of wisdom into my new world. This division manager could see I needed help and guided me gently from the side, preventing me from stumbling.

Making mental notes to prepare for my next meeting, I had to be on top all the time, had to be brilliant and ahead of the wave at a moment's notice. It was exhausting. I hoped my kids would call more often. I needed to have their reassurance, just to hear their voices, but weeks went by and only if I called them did I hear their news. I had tried to be so independent, maybe they couldn't see past my brave façade. To them, I guess I was still their strong and competent mother and didn't need their help. I had created this image and now had to think through stuff alone. Late at night, in my tiny rented room, these thoughts raced through my dark, awake dreams. Out loud I said, "You need to pull in all your creative energy, have your old confidence back, don't be lured into self-doubt." I pushed the dark fragments away and drifted off to sleep.

50

Anne

My personal angel continued to hover over me during this transition period, and while being introduced to the many area management people in some of the surrounding cafeterias, I met Anne. She was a manager in charge of a small Guckenheimer contract in the Bay area. I felt from the first meeting she would be a major influence in my new life. That day the air was charged with anticipation; a sign post for positive things ahead. She radiated good will.

We both talked at once saying, "We should meet after work for drinks and conversation." It was exciting to meet someone near my age and in a similar business, a possible new friend. Exchanging phone numbers, we promised to call soon.

A week later we met at a trendy bistro and talked our hearts out all through appetizers, entrees and dessert. We were both from the Pacific Northwest, she was from Seattle, I was from Vancouver, she was divorced, and I was widowed.

I said," Anne, I'm thinking ahead to renting a flat in the city, but I need to consider a roommate. I'm not sure if I can handle all the rent, the job is so new and all. Are you on your own? Maybe we could be roomies?" It was a big chance that all would be smooth. I'd heard a lot of horror stories about roommates, but we were adults not kids in college.

Anne said, "Can we meet at my apartment in Redwood City on Saturday? Maybe this might work out. I've been thinking of moving to the Bay area but the opportunity just wasn't there, now maybe…" her voice drifted off.

At her apartment, Anne got more excited visualizing our future, throwing out suggestions as fast as she could speak. We had so much in common it was scary.

My second life began with Anne helping me to adjust and grow into my new Corporate World. We were so attuned that when we unpacked our boxes, we had the same books, dishes, cutlery and furniture. We each had a copy of Sailing in the Pacific Northwest and Puget Sound.

I said, "You were sailors too? My husband and I had a thirty three foot Swedish sailboat for ten years." Anne, her husband and children had also sailed the same waters for years. The similarities just appeared everywhere.

A pact was formed that if either of us had furniture that did not fit our new spaces, we would talk about it first, then put whatever it was in storage or just give it away. This was not the time to just make-do! Two Saturdays later after house hunting all over San Francisco we found a perfect flat near the Golden Gate Park.

Our new home was going to be chic, comfortable and inviting, with soft upholstered couches, have fresh flowers and potpourri. Décor was our favorite word. After settling in, we planned an extravagant Open House for friends and business associates. We even hired valet parking for our guests, which we highlighted on our party invitations. We knew how hard it was to find parking anywhere in the city.

To create the right image this was our list. First, the food. Not just chips and dip but real food that people in our business would expect. We wrote down many ideas but this was the final menu, the 'Right Stuff' for us.

Slivers of Smoked Duck Breast with Chutney
Crusty Baguettes/Baby Rolls
Deep Fried Ravioli
Mushroom Tartlets
Baron of Beef with Creamy Horseradish
Shrimp and Rice New Orleans
Paisley Salad
Petite Rhubarb Pastries,
Chocolate Imperialé Flourless Cake, drenched in Chocolate Ganache
Orange Bavarian Torte

Picture this…Pots of white cyclamen on all thirty stairs, three flights up, to our flat floating above the city. Huge containers of white hydrangea blooms in all the rooms set the scene. Dozens of gold and silver balloons floated up on the twelve foot ceilings with long silver ribbons trailing. Champagne flutes on silver trays and our extravagant buffet of food in the dining room. Everything -sparkled on silver and glass trays among the décor of green vines and white flowers. Valet parking was a perk. How extravagant! It was a splendid start, s-o-o-o-o San Francisco. We were pleased with our launch. When the last guests waved good-by, we snacked on some of the tasty leftovers while gathering up the plates and glasses and exclaimed, "What a great party!"

ORANGE BAVARIAN TORTE

I was still relying on my cache of ethnic recipes for support. This is one of my best cake delicacies. This Torte is an example of the creative use of ingredients using cake and jam for that different effect around the cake edge. Techniques like this are used by accomplished pastry chefs. You now know how to do it too.

Preheat oven 450 about 7 minutes
Parchment paper
Sheet pan
10"spring form pan
Serves 8-10
Medium

Sheet Cake
4 egg yolks
4 whole eggs
1 cup generous sugar

5 egg whites
1½ Tbsp. sugar

¾ cup sifted flour
1 tsp. baking powder

Method
Beat first 3 ingredients together until light.
Beat next whites together, slowly at first. then add sugar and beat on medium.

Add sifted flour into yolks.

Take a scoop of whites to lighten the mixture, then fold in all the whites.

Spread onto parchment lined sheet pan, 11x17.

Bake in middle of the oven about 7 minutes or until lightly browned.

Turn out onto cake rack, leave paper on until ready to use. Cover with a towel. Cool.

Cut a circle of cake the size of the bottom of a 9" spring form pan. Remove paper.

Spread the rest of the cake with apricot jam. Remove bottom paper. Cut strips of cake 2" wide, (the height of your spring form pan), and 17 inches long.

Pile strips of 4 or 5 on top of one another. Wrap in saran and place in freezer to make slicing easier. These will be used to decoratively edge cake pan later.

Orange Cream

2 large oranges, zest plus juice
2 Tbsp. sugar
7 egg yolks
1 cup sugar
2 tsp cornstarch
1½ cups simmering milk.
2 packages plain gelatin

5 egg whites
1 Tbsp. sugar

Method

Mix zest of oranges with sugar, set aside.

In a standing mixer bowl, add orange/zest sugar to yolks.

Add the rest of sugar, cornstarch until well blended.
Add hot milk in a thin stream, then add all to saucepan and
thicken over medium heat.
Squeeze orange juice to make ½ cup juice. Sprinkle gelatin
over to soften.
Add gelatin mixture to above custard cream, whisking for a
few moments to dissolve completely.
Beat whites, adding 1 Tbsp. sugar and beat to stiff peaks.
Fold into <u>hot custard</u>. Set in refrigerator. Spoon mixture
several times while cooling to keep custard well blended and
smooth. **<u>When cold but not completely set, proceed.</u>**

1 cup chilled whipped cream
2 Tbsp. orange liqueur

Beat cream and liqueur to soft peaks. Fold lightly into above
cooled custard.

¼ cup strong tea
⅛ cup Grand Marnier

<u>Assembly</u>
Lightly oil inside of spring form pan, (one 10" or two 7").
Cut cake strips ¼" thick, and turn on end to line inside edge
of pan.
Pour Bavarian Cream into center.
Paint cake circle with tea/liqueur and place on top, (this will
be the bottom when unmolded).
Let set up 3 hours or over-night. Perfect for making ahead.

Congratulations, you have managed the whole recipe. Seems long but is really easy when taken in parts. This cake is delicately flavored and impressive. Friends will ask how you created the decorative edge.

Barbara J Miachika

RHUBARB BUTTER TARTS

Using Rhubarb is a little surprise and is a nice tart/sweet filling. I found it interesting that some people didn't even know what Rhubarb was.

Bake 425 approx. 15 minutes, then lower to 376 10 more.

2 cup fresh Rhubarb, cut in ½" pieces
½ cup soft butter
½ cup brown sugar
½ tsp. salt
1 cup corn syrup
2 eggs, lightly beaten
24 tart shells, unbaked

Method
Scald rhubarb, let stand in water 5 minutes, drain. Press with spoon in strainer, to get out excess water.
In a medium bowl, mix sugar, butter and salt, add corn syrup. Add rhubarb and mix gently.
Add eggs. Fold all together.
Fill tart shells ⅔ full, (don't over fill as the mixture can stick to the tart tin and break pastry when removing from the tin.
Bake 15 minutes at 425, then 375 for 10 minutes more until bubbly and nicely browned.

51
The UC Berkeley Rose Arbor

I was so busy with new experiences I didn't have time to miss my children or my mother but did they miss me? I hoped so.

Anne and I shared life together for the next six years. We were both diligent about our work, for me building on a career, for her only a job right now, her field was really psychology. (The owner of Guckenheimer, Stewart Ritchie 111, was her brother-in-law, and had made a temporary place for her as a unit manager until her chosen field presented itself.) We had many late night discussions about Guckenheimer, her position within her family and the direction of our lives. It was good for each of us to have a safe sounding board.

So many events fight for space spanning this time in my life, but the following vignettes influenced the threads of my life from completely different angles.

The prospect of new friends under the guise of a rustic picnic at the Rose Arbor Garden on the Berkeley campus in Oakland, made us spring into action. A friend of a friend had invited us, the two foodies, to be part of this fun day. Altogether there would be ten guests, a mixed bag. We of course were to bring the food, while the rest would supply drinks, plates, cutlery, glasses, a blanket and music.

Anne said, "Whatever we bring it has to be impressive." Obvious! Duh!

As usual, the menu just jumped into my head, "This will be the right stuff," and I continued to ramble off my suggestions faster than I could write them down. The soup would be transported in a thermos, the rest traveled in baskets. The textures and flavors all worked well. Here is the menu.

<u>The Rose Arbor Picnic</u>

My Own Antipasto,
(from Vancouver)
Nuggets of Breaded Pigs Feet
later called "Chicken Knees"
Hot Roasted Tomato Soup
Lentil/White Bean Salad
Potato Salad en Gelé
Crusty Baguettes
Mini Soufflés of Nouvelle Bread Pudding
Nanaimo Bars

The real reason the picnic remains memorable for me was Ludwig, one of the guests; an interesting single gentleman, very attractive, slim, mischievous deep blue eyes, my age, and he drove an Italian convertible. The day was perfect.

The food consumed, the drink cooler emptied, and as dusk approached, the return trip back to my place across the Golden Gate Bridge in San Francisco was in his two- seater car. It seemed tinged with possibilities. Would he call next week or ever?

Over the next seven years, I did see Ludwig quite a bit. He was a laser scientist employed by one of those technical companies in the Silicon Valley. He was fun, well-educated and had an intriguing German accent. We had a serious romance and I was enamoured with him but he never really committed to anything for sure, he couldn't say, "I love you," and mean it. Somehow I could tell it was insincere. If only I had remembered my mother's best dating advice from long ago; don't be too available, be a little mysterious and don't give all of yourself until you are sure. If I had remembered this advice it might have ended differently. In any case it ended.

ANTI-PASTO

Having a few jars of Anti Pasto in reserve is a smart way to entertain whenever guests drop in. I had arrived in San Francisco with some of my stash from Vancouver, so I put two jars in the picnic basket for our Rose Garden affair. (A bit time consuming, but worth the results.)

24 pint jars, scalded and drained onto a tea towel.

Medium

2 lb. silver skin onions
2 medium zucchini
2 large cauliflowers
6 celery stalks
4 lb. bell peppers, red and green
2 ½ lb. mushrooms
2 lb. carrots
1 lb. cucumbers
32 oz. olive oil
20 oz. white vinegar
1 tin green olives, small
3 tins black olives, pitted
1 tin pimento olives
3 lb. green beans
1 large tin tomato paste
1 large bottle ketchup
4 tins anchovies
5 large tins tuna, good quality, solid white

2 large bottles chilli sauce
1 ½ tsp. salt

Method

Clean and chop vegetables into bite size pieces, (not too small).
Put oil and vinegar into a very large stock pot and bring to a boil.
Add tomato paste, ketchup and chilli sauce.
Boil 5 minutes. Add salt.
<u>Add in this order</u>
Carrots, and celery, boil 5 minutes.
Beans, boil 5 minutes.
Cukes and mushrooms, boil 5 minutes.
Cauliflower, boil 10 minutes.
Peppers, and zucchini, boil 5 minutes.
Add anchovies, silver skin onions and olives.

Drain tuna and break into chunky pieces. Place one piece in the bottom of each sterilized jar, adding lids per directions on box for how tight to turn down, and steam in water bath 20 minutes.
When filling jars, leave ½" at top.
Wipe edges of jar clean before adding lid and ring. It will keep almost indefinitely.
Enjoy.

NANAIMO BARS, CANADIAN SWEET

There really is a place called Nanaimo. It is a town on Vancouver Island, up the inner coastline from Victoria. This mixture has been around for quite a long time and now even Food Service distributors sell it.
Many new flavours have been added, but this one is the original.

Easy
1 large, commercial size sheet pan, (22x34)
4 cups unsalted butter
2 cups sugar
¾ cup cocoa
4 eggs
1½ tsp. vanilla

Method
Use a large stainless bowl over simmering water.
Whisk first three ingredients together over hot water until butter is melted and all blended.
Remove from heat, stir in eggs, vanilla, blend.

Add to same bowl
8 cups crushed graham wafer cookies
4 cups fine shredded unsweetened coconut (health food or bulk food -stores)
2 cups chopped nuts, almonds, hazelnuts or walnuts

Blend well and press onto sheet pan, spread plastic over surface pressing mixture with fingers to create firm base.

Mix

1 cup soft butter
8 cups icing sugar sifted
½ cup dry Bird's Eye Vanilla custard powder. (2 packets) or other vanilla brand custard mix, blended with ¾ cup milk.
Mix well, spread over crumb base.
Chill.

Melt

8 squares semi-sweet chocolate in stainless bowl over simmering water
8 squares bitter chocolate
¼ cup butter
Spread over chilled custard base.
Refrigerate to firm up chocolate glaze.

Cut into 2" squares with a sharp chef knife. This bar travels well for sailing, picnics or parties.
Note. Recipes can be cut in half, using ½ size sheet pan.

52
My Mother

San Francisco is a wonderful city to live in at any stage of life. Anne and I experienced so many different enriching arts available to anyone willing to expend the energy to take part. Through a friend, we were able to be part of a chosen group "Ushering the Boxes" at the San Francisco Ballet. It is a hidden treat known only to a few, that one can see the ballet for free after completing the ushering duties. The 'Boxes" are the most prestigious seats, located on the second level and are sold by the season or held year to year by the upper crust and therefore the most interesting clientele. It felt good to be part of the elegant crowd and not have to pay for it. At Christmas one had to agree to usher at least five performances of the Nutcracker, (it was repeated so many times), that after one or two it got pretty boring but it made the rest of the season's ballet program a bargain.

But back to my Christmas story.

My Mother, a widow now for several years, was always sent a plane ticket to San Clemente in southern California, to visit my sister Sherle and brother-in-law Arthur for the Christmas season. This was their present to her. I called Sherle to suggest an open -jaw fare to allow a stop-over for no extra cost, in San Francisco to visit me.

Sherle said, "Great idea, Mother will love it". On her last trip she was having trouble walking, so she might be in a wheel chair coming out of the jet way. Arthur and I see her aging now, more on each trip."

I was excited to have her with me for a few days, to let her see my surroundings, to know I was okay in my new life, and to meet Anne, my roommate, someone I had mentioned quite a bit each time I phoned my mother. I planned a special brunch to celebrate the occasion. I also invited my friend Betty, my girlfriend from years before in Vancouver that I hoped Mother might remember. As an added surprise I hired a quartet of costumed carollers to appear as if by chance at our door. We were all seated in the dining room. The bell rang. I jumped up to answer it coyly saying, "Who could that possibly be?"

Merrily attired in winter hats and mufflers, with tinkling bells on their costumes, they arrived on queue and proceeded to serenade us for an hour from the archway to the dining room, filling the air with Christmas songs in French, German and English, sung *a-cappella*. Tears came to us all as they sang "O Christmas Tree," in English, then German, prompting a favourite memory from my grade three pageant; where with my proud parents watching, I sang the same carol wrapped in green cellophane holding a star. This was a magical moment in time.

Mother said, "How amazing that they appeared here today. I can still see you as a little tree, waving that star and singing so sweetly." She had no idea!

I just winked at Betty and Anne and the secret was ours.

AUNT FAYE'S CHRISTMAS CAKE

Aunt Faye was not my real aunt but her fame continues on with this remarkable combination of whole fruit and nuts to produce one of the easiest and most delicious Christmas concoctions. Aunt Faye did know a few things about baking. This cake is mostly fruit and nuts, not much cake. Well wrapped it keeps for months, (if there is any left), in the refrigerator. When cut in thin slices, it was the perfect addition to our Christmas luncheon.

Preheat oven. Bake 300 for 1 hour and 45 minutes
Easy

1 lb. shelled Brazil nuts
1 lb. pitted dates
1 cup glace red cherries
¾ cup flour
¾ cup sugar
½ tsp. baking powder
½ tsp. salt
3 eggs
1 tsp. vanilla
1 tsp. black walnut extract

Method
Put nuts and cherries in a large bowl.
Sift flour, sugar, baking powder and salt over nuts and fruit to coat.
Beat eggs and add flavourings, add to bowl.
Turn over with wooden spoon to mix well.

Scrape into prepared greased, lined with parchment, 4x13 loaf pan of choice.
Spread evenly; press down to eliminate any clusters or holes.
Bake. This makes 1- 3lb loaf.

53
Club Med

Working twelve hour days, pulling energy from my past, I struggled in the trenches to give Guckenheimer my all. I was not used to being tied to a week-day schedule. The first year went past so fast I had to remember to rip the months from my calendar. After one year of work, I was desperately in need of some fun, just fun! One week's vacation was all I was due, but where to go?

Club Med seemed the best bet for the money and Anne agreed to go too. Safety in numbers. However when it was time, her commitments held her back, so I arrived at the airport alone and apprehensive. Everyone at the jet-way oozed sex: They all had trim young bodies. Club Med began.

But surprise, surprise, I need not have doubted myself! The trip was all I could have hoped for in one week. I was transported into the current mode of the game. Food and drink was a good starting point mixed with sun, surf and body contact. Hardly believing, I was thrilled and astounded at my new sexual power, my hormones that had lain dormant for several years thundered into action. I was fifty-six and he was thirty- four, but I felt eighteen!

Several nights that week, my young female roommate didn't see me until the next morning.

She'd say, "You go girl," and give me a wink and high five.

I returned to work revived and ready for anything. You bet I could hardly wait to share my juicy conquests with Anne, my best girlfriend, and confidante.

At work I had many challenges each week, dashing from one account to the next to work with staff and managers on all aspects of the production. It seemed everything needed to be revamped; décor, signage, product, training, sanitation issues and general productivity. I was a human Band-Aid! I drove to most locations in my own mini-van, a useful carry-all. I really needed a company car like the other upper level managers. But three requests to my supervisor so far produced zero. Hmmm!

When Anne would arrive home after her day's work, exhausted, I was already baking a cake or some type of dessert, a relaxing mechanism for me, producing immediate gratification and something tangible for my effort.

"Had a stressful day?" she would ask. "What delicious treats will we be having for dessert tonight?"

A lot of people thought Anne and I were sisters, two peas in a pod. We did look quite a bit alike, so we just played it up and enjoyed our professional life together. This was one lucky part of my new direction to be thankful for, to have such a great roommate when it could've been really awful. All these facets pointed me in the right direction in my new city.

54

My Perfect Car

I had worked for Guckenheimer for three years and it was going quite well. I was accumulating a nest egg. My life there gave me some kudos and a cheque for my effort every week. My children were into their own lives and were happy that I was independent and carrying on, overcoming such a rocky ending in Vancouver. But by taking this direction, moving to San Francisco, I was not able to be part of my grandchildren's lives. To be the perfect grandma was not in the cards for me. I would miss their growing years. I had to look at it all in perspective. My immediate goal was to be self-sufficient and survive. I could not worry about the long-term results right now.

My work engulfed all my thoughts. I continued to keep ahead of the competition with creative ideas applying my all for Guckenheimer foods and menus.

Standing back, I wondered how I was doing. I said to Anne, "Sometimes I feel so alone. Is this the right place for me?" I doubted myself now that I had time to be retrospective. The corporate world had so many layers. Was I fitting in?

She said, "Can you see yourself doing this for the next ten years?" She was pushing me to step out of the 'weeds' and take a good look. Her psychology background was showing through.

"Maybe as long as I have the energy," I said. It was impossible for me to imagine my body without my signature high energy. I was in my late fifty's, very fit, not allowing myself to page forward. I always seemed inexhaustible. Was energy the fear of the matter? Or was it something else?

I said, "If I could delegate more, it would help, but so much of what I did was my own signature look, not something easily passed on. Something as simple as a helper loading the van for each project would be a start." I needed to speak up more. But was that really the stickler?

I thought back to my recent performance review where I had all pluses; however three requests for a small company car were ignored. I was being too polite!

My subconscious emotions niggled my brain to reveal the real problem. There was something about my ego at work here. The mention of the van forced me to face a conundrum. I didn't like the game my supervisors were playing. Their refusal to grant me a company car said loud and clear, "You are not on our level." It was the Good Old Boys flexing their muscles. I had the title but not he clout. My inexperience in the corporate world was showing. How to get what I wanted?

My inner voice said, "Think like a man. Buy your own car, maybe a sports car, and sell your fucking van! Learn to work the system." I plotted my next moves.

Driving the many freeways to each job in my van during the next months, I started to notice what my next car should be. A Porsche would be perfect. After doing my research it was narrowed down to the 911 S Targa with its classic shape. Not new, of course, I couldn't afford that, but it would be a second-hand model in excellent shape. I would spot a Porsche in traffic; get a lump in my throat and a shot of adrenaline.

Betty, my long-time friend said, "If you don't stop talking about that car I will scream. Just buy the damm thing or shut up."

An ad under Autos in the local paper read…

Silver Porsche, good condition,

911 S, Targa, Marin.

Make an offer

<u>Must Sell</u>

The next day I drove over the Golden Gate Bridge to Mill Valley in Marin. I picked my way through the winding streets, climbing the hillside until I came to the correct address. The garage door rolled up and there it was, glistening, poised, just waiting for me. I tried to act cool almost forgetting to breathe. I went through my check list with the owner.

"Test-drive it around the block," he cagily suggested. He backed my prize out onto the roadway, a throbbing, silver insect. The driver's door was ajar for me to slide inside. I could smell the aroma of leather, black, even before sitting down.

Of course I was hooked and made the commitment right then. The next day, at lunch-hour, downtown, we met. I exchanged my money for his car keys. How easy was that! I was now the owner of my wildest dream, a classic Porsche! This car was too small for most bulky décor but room enough for my starched chef jacket, my tool box of knives and a bag of last minute fresh parsley or basil. I was assertive. I was cheeky. I got away with it. Mission accomplished.

FRESH OYSTERS WITH MIGNIONETTE SAUCE

This is a chic hors d'oeuvre to serve a lucky guest after a ride in my Porsche. This will make a memorable evening served with cold, crisp champagne.

Easy, if you know how to shuck oysters.

2 dz. fresh, small oysters: opened, saving the liquid, resting in the half shell.

Sauce
White peppercorns, crushed
1 Tbsp. sugar
1 cup rice wine vinegar
2 Tbsp. olive oil
1 shallot, minced
1 Tbsp. fresh ginger, minced, very important
½ tsp. red pepper flakes
Fresh cracked black pepper

Method
Whisk above ingredients to blend.
Reserve and chill.

Assembly
Plate oysters on bed of coarse salt.
Place ramekin of Mignonette sauce on same platter with small spoon. Let guests help themselves slurping juices right from shell to mouth.

55
33 Beideman St

I was so ecstatic about the prospect of a new house. Was it really possible that I could buy my own home? To have a house again was on my long wish list.

Anne and I had now lived together in San Francisco for six years but we each knew and felt it was still only a transition period. However the years had continued to slip by. I would fantasize about my dream home and therefore the necessity for a housewarming party The menu would drift into my thoughts; seared baby lamb chops, smoked turkey, mini jalapeño corn muffins with chutney, lobster salad, Arugula greens tossed with toasted pine nuts and juicy pomegranate kernels, large rounds of French cheeses, pates set out on my butcher block in the kitchen and of course one of my fabulous chocolate/pastry cakes, the recipe from my catering company in West Vancouver "The Right Stuff Catering)." Even the guest list appeared in my head and all would be perfect.

My friend Betty thought it was the funniest reason she had ever heard of for anyone wanting to purchase a house. It became a joke in all our conversations. She said, "Let me know when you find the right place, I'm ready for a party."

The real estate market in California was at low ebb, but this was only helpful if you had the ability to gather the down payment. However, when there is a desire it can become a reality. After seven months of house hunting week-ends, I fell in love with a small Victorian building available on a quiet street in the city. At this same time, a lump sum of cash arrived from David, my lawyer son. He had concluded a final bank settlement from Anton's muddied financial affairs, with the Canadian government, His efforts in court reaped this cash windfall in our favor, and the three boys divided it up four ways, including me.

I called Anthony in Vancouver to fly down and have a look at this piece of real estate. I valued his business sense. He echoed my enthusiasm when we viewed the property.

With a ten percent down payment, I made a low but clean offer. Several days later I was the owner of this exotic property.

The rooms were filled with light from the tall "Italianate" windows; 12 foot ceilings, a marble fireplace with a gas jet, French doors leading out from a perfect small kitchen to raised deck and cobble stoned back parking with private landscaped garden. You knew it would have a perfect kitchen with a gas stove. I could hardly wait to phone Betty to tell her that I was going to be moving into my own home and for her to start thinking about what she would wear to my party.

No more reminiscing about my former fabulous home in West Vancouver. It had faded into the past. This new purchase was a building block toward my future. I had regained some of my footing. My wish list was working its magic. All these events helped propel me forward.

MINI JALAPEÑOS CORN MUFFINS

Here is a perfect addition to any food buffet.
Lots of other ingredients can be added for flavor
changes.

Easy
Makes 24 mini muffins
Oven 350
2 mini muffin pans

1 box Corn muffin mix, Follow directions on box.
2 slices cooked bacon, crumbled.
½ cup fresh, frozen corn kernels, thawed.
¼ cup sour cream
Finely grated fresh ginger.
Shredded cheddar cheese
1 jalapeños pepper, minced fine

<u>Method</u>
Mix according to box directions.
Add above extra ingredients. Check for texture.
Drop by Tbsp. into sprayed tins. Don't over fill.
Bake 8-10 minutes until lightly browned and risen to top .
Cool on rack.
Serve in a small basket with purchased chutney.

56

Romance in the Kitchen

My middle son Paul, with his usual clear and to the point style asked, "If you should lose your job, how will you afford this mortgage?" That had not been part of my original equation as I felt firmly ensconced in my position as Merchandising and Marketing Specialist for ARA, an international food service company that had head hunted me into this new position. I was confident as I looked optimistically to the future.

With all this in mind any renovations to my charming house had to be carefully considered, meaning done for the least possible cost or not at all.

How do people find each other at the right time? It seems a coincident but is it? Do inner signals seem to float through the air like silent radio waves or perhaps a chubby cupid takes pity on you and strikes with his arrow, temporarily stunning the senses?

A year ago, Douglas and I met at a Home Show as I was perusing all the displays. He had a stall for his construction company. When I chatted about my needs and wants for my home, Douglas gallantly suggested he could perhaps take a look and fit in a few hours between his other work and I could do some catering to promote new clients for him. It was all a marketing thing. Maybe he could already smell the possibility of future dinners or maybe he liked the whole package: my blue eyes and friendly smile.

One Sunday, after several visits and a start on some of the work, Douglas was in the back garden finishing the outdoor lighting. The evening hour was almost dusk, and soft shadows were falling amongst the leaves from the branches of the trees, the new twinkling mini lights creating stars swirling down the thick tree trunk to the ground. My place looked like Tavern on the Green in Central Park.

Dinner of seared duck breast with brandied cherries was almost ready and the aroma enveloped the kitchen. He caught me by surprise, quietly returning from the garden, stepping into the kitchen behind me and pressing a first kiss to the nape of my neck! How seductive! I was taken completely by surprise. What was this long forgotten lusty desire that encircled my very soul? I succumbed to the flash and unexpected thrill of it all, quivering like an ally cat's tail; my legs were jelly! He had ignited a pit of flames, long ago snuffed out. I fell completely into him, not even trying to save myself. And so it began.

Still in San Francisco and on my own, it felt good to have someone special help me launch this new home, create fairy lighting in the garden, add new plugs where there originally were none, hang my 350 pound pot rack and devour my candlelight dinners while we shared intimate kisses. Douglas loved having someone special need him too, appreciate his talents for renovation, his billiard technique, his dry humor, his odd poetry, his young energy, his tempting kisses and more. At thirty-nine he had many special talents.

I continued to accept catering jobs and one was a benefit for the San Francisco Food Society, to raise money for the food bank in the city. I donated 250 Lemon Curd Tarts. On that sunny Sunday, Douglas helped me set up my table in the garden of an historic mansion over in East Bay. I had my mixer plugged into a tree, yes a tree, and I finished filling the tarts on site. What a funny picture, my mixer cord plugged into a tree, (there was an outlet there)! This was all new for him. He was useful at times and added to the fun. The romance lasted 9 months.

The pain of it all…can I really live another day alone…again? I think men don't feel the rejection and sadness when separation happens. I guess this was the risk of allowing me to feel…I gave part of myself away. It was time for chocolate.

Even though this relationship ended badly, on reflection and much soul searching, there was much that was valuable and worked for each of us during that time. We had touched each other's lives whether we wanted to admit it or not.

Added to my own lifestyle, I was now a devoted billiards player. Also encouraged by Douglas, I began to pen my autobiography. He stepped out of his box to enjoy the symphony as much as his favorite "The Doors," was the proud owner of his first Porsche car and tried to become a Gourmand. I knew he wasn't really the one for me but…he had that something!

When things fall apart you wonder if it would have been better to not risk your heart, eat peanut butter sandwiches alone, read romance novels and spend your evening visiting your mother. No, better that you choose to be alive, accept the good shots to fall your way, be a little wild, and then let yourself feel special and know that you are!

After the break-up I baked, cleaned, vacuumed and generally worked myself into exhaustion: I kept physically busy. The winner was my house. It sparkled.

BARBARA'S HOUSE TRUFFELS

These truffles will always heal any crisis. Deep, dark, smooth chocolate centers dusted on the outside in bitter cocoa, will wash away persistent angry thoughts, leaving room for maybe one more bite.

Easy

Ganache
1 cup heavy cream
12 oz. dark semi-sweet chocolate, chopped
6Tbsp. un-salted butter
2Tbsp. liqueur, maybe grand Marnier or rum Splash vanilla

1½ lb. chocolate for over-dipping or roll truffles in unsweetened baking cocoa.

Method
Over medium low, heat cream, do not boil. Remove, cream, add chopped chocolate and chopped, unsalted butter and blend to a smooth mixture and all is melted.
Add flavorings. Pour into shallow pan or container to chill in refrigerator and firm up.
Scoop with melon ball or tablespoon, chill again.
Melt dipping chocolate over hot water, tempering if necessary to prevent 'bloom'
Dip centers using a two pronged fork, swirling to thread over top surface for design. Refrigerate to harden.
Other garnishes; Chocolate covered coffee beans, Candied ginger, lemon rind, angelica or candied violets.

57

Mark Hopkins Hotel, San Francisco

The Intercontinental Mark Hopkins Hotel, San Francisco, is a member of the group known as The Big Four. The others are, The Huntington, The Fairmont and The Stanford Court, all glamorous landmarks in downtown San Francisco. Opened in 1926, and located at 1 Nob Hill, the 'Mark' with its nineteen floors presides over the city in grand style. The elevator opens on the top floor into The Sky Lounge, a glamorous destination for beaux to impress their dates with exquisite dining, dancing to sophisticated music and a glass or two of champagne. Fabulous, breathtaking views of the city, the Golden Gate Bridge and the Marin Headlands!

I was a member of several prominent food associations related to my business. At one of the extravagant monthly dinners held by the I.W.F.S, (the International Wine and Food Society), I was by chance seated next to a charming gentleman who turned out to be the new General Manager of the Mark Hopkins Hotel. As we chatted between courses, he discovered that I had owned my own cooking school ten years previous.

He said, "Because you have the marketing skills for that success, would you be interested in creating a cooking school at the Mark Hopkins?" He felt the time was ripe but wasn't sure how to get it off the ground nor did he have the time to devote to it, but he wanted to work with the chef on the idea. "Could you work with the Executive Chef, plan ahead with him, discuss seasonal menus, and work as a liaison between guests during the class?"

"Yes, that would be fun," I replied, with nervous excitement in my voice. I set up a time in the next week to meet with his staff, Chef Ward Little, the restaurant manager, Frank Carrola and the Mark's marketing team in their office. Of course I was thrilled at the prestige of it all. I could already see the new credentials on my resume. Anne would be so impressed at my good luck!

At the Mark, I settled myself into a soft leather chair in the hushed inner office of the marketing group. After introductions all around, the Mark's restaurant manager, Frank Carrola, the two-person marketing team and I got down to business.

They outlined the best day of the week regarding the chef's available time and the best time for kitchen space.

Frank said, "Saturday AM was the best all around; for the Chef and possibly for the guests. Was it good for me?"

"Saturday was perfect for me," I said. My every-day food service job was mostly Monday to Friday usually leaving Saturday open.

They sat back and said, "You can have carte blanche with the rest of the details as you have done this before. Bring in your plan and we will create a press release and menu sheets. My name, included at the bottom of each sheet said, Recipe and Menu Culinary Consultant, Barbara Miachika, paired with Chef Ward Little. Amazing! No monetary compensation up front for me but I would receive gratis, evenings of dining for two and wonderful exposure in the culinary arena. Everyone was pleased.

Notices about the new venture appeared on the hotel web site as well as in a formal mailer. Professionally printed and presented in a gold envelope, the Mark Hopkins Cooking School was launched. It took quite a few afternoon meetings between Ward and me for us both to feel comfortable working together.

My enticing, visual wording on the brochure, described the inner sanctum of the big kitchen, *vis-à-vis* with the head chef, Ward Little, then lunch with white table cloth service in the dining room, silver, and crystal wine glasses was all spelled out on a formal card for reservations. The idea was well received. Right away we had twelve confirmed; some for the whole series for $320, a few just for one class at $85, (those were guests staying at the hotel and unsure how long they were staying). The price was not a problem.

We planned to meet at 10 AM at the entrance to the dining room, to be led down a back entry by the Maître d' to the huge kitchen a floor below. There the chef would be waiting. Once we were all gathered around his station, my first job was to hand out the day's menu enclosed in a folder enhanced with a beautiful watercolor of the hotel's front garden. Inside, pink parchment sheets with today's recipes gave us a clue for what was to come.

The day of the first class arrived. We gathered around the chef's station, waiting expectantly for the Wizard to speak.

He said, "Today's menu will reflect our coming season, using the freshest ingredients." He went on to elaborate…

"Foie Gras with Golden Apple Puree,
Fresh Sea Bass from the Market with Chanterelles
Roast Squab with Macaroni Gratin/Oregano au Jus
(the pièce de resistance)
Double Chocolate Dome with Gold Leaf

As a group, we were off to a good start! The chef in his traditional whites had a quiet, almost shy, personality so it was perfect for me to enhance his explanations as he worked, for me to interact giving additional explanations to the students. First on the plate was Foie Gras. This was a mysterious item for the students, to see it raw and to understand how to handle it. He got everyone's attention saying, "This is how to dissect this expensive, raw treat. Carefully take the veins and threadlike arteries from the fatty globe with a small knife, and then it will be ready to slice into single portions to sauté. See how it's shaped into two sections. This succulent prize will be our first course."

Someone said, "I could never do that."

"Yes you can, now that you have all the tricks and you know where to buy it," I countered.

How to peel potatoes to make perfect ovals intrigued everyone. Murmurs from a student, whispering how he was ready to invite his friends to his next soiree using this menu, was encouraging. The class continued. The students loved it!

We weren't finished yet. Chef Little described the nuances of the next courses. About the Sea Bass, holding up a whole fresh fish, he pointed out the eyes saying, "See the clear eyes, this is a good way to know if it is fresh. Fish should always smell of the sea, a clear briny aroma."

Once the details were accomplished, he waved his hand for all to follow him down another elevator to arrive in the basement. This was the pastry chef's domain and he handed the class over to her, hurrying back to his morning duties.

Windows all across one side of the structure brought in natural light. It was an unglamorous, concrete space but the pastries and desserts transformed it. Oh. the aromas, it smelled wonderful. There were cakes and pastries everywhere. It was Willi Wonka's workshop. It made me almost dizzy. I was in my glory.

Lorri Raji, the Executive Pastry Chef, stood behind a huge marble slab, her work table. She was ready for us in her crisp white apron and tall hat. Off to one side, commercial ovens dispensed dozens of shortbread cookies for today's dessert plates for the dining room. Unusual machines and hundreds of pans and tart shells of different shapes waited on shelves wherever you looked. Away from the bustle, an amazing five- tier wedding cake received the finishing top layer from a talented icing artist.

Lorri gathered us in. She read the recipe out loud for us and explained how everything would come together.

She said, "Always read the entire recipe first. Make sure you have all the ingredients and correct pans in front of you." (In my school, I said these same words to my students). She showed us the steps needed to melt the Belgian chocolate, whip the whites and fold them together. "Remember to allow enough time to chill the mixture before proceeding, chill in the fridge for two or more hours in the pan."

She continued, "The trick here was to have a rectangular pan two inches deep, of the right length to use a #10 potato scoop to draw it across the mousse to form perfect scoops. Release onto a sheet pan, and then freeze them for at least one hour. When ready, lift the required number of domes onto a cake rack; drape melted chocolate over each one, letting the excess fall onto parchment underneath. Place a flake of gold leaf on your finger and affix it on top. Center the glistening mousse dome on a dessert plate and drizzle Custard Crème Anglaise around the edges. Add a shortbread cookie on the edge of the plate. Dust with Icing Sugar."

She said with a flourish, "This is one of my signature sweets for the dining room, Double Chocolate Mousse Dome with Gold Leaf." She made it look so easy. Everyone clapped, now anxious to get to the dining room upstairs and experience the spoils.

We trooped along the back corridors stepping over wires and avoiding carts, until the light in the dining room reappeared, showing us the way. There, waiting for us was the head waiter, all crisp and smiling, ready to serve us the results of our morning class.

The wine was poured; the Foie Gras appeared, napped with its delicious sauce, looking entirely different, touched by chef's magic. Just a short time ago, it was a raw blob on the counter. Now it was a heavenly morsel in our mouths.

While we sipped and ate, it was up to me to 'talk up' the future classes. Most of the students immediately signed up for next production, not even knowing what was coming. The manager was pleased; for the Chef it was all in a day's work. It was fun for me. I was impressed. The hotel dining room would now get the attention it deserved.

MARK HOPKINS DOUBLE CHOCOLATE DOME WITH GOLD LEAF

This special dessert was made by the pastry chef at the Mark Hopkins Hotel. I was the coordinator for this special Cooking School. Do try it! It is smooth, delicious and impressive. Honey is the special ingredient.

Medium

5 egg yolks
2 oz. honey
½ lb. semi-sweet Belgian chocolate, melted
2 ¾ cups heavy cream

Method
Beat yolks in mixer until light colored
In a small saucepan bring honey to a boil and cook on high for 2 minutes,
Then add to yolks in a stream, avoid mixer blades
Add melted chocolate
Whip cream to medium soft peaks, fold whites into chocolate/egg mixture, blend but do not overwork
Pour into a 2 inch deep hotel pan, (3x8x2) and chill for several hours
Use a #10 potato scoop and place domes on a wire rack and put in the freezer to keep hard before glazing.

Glaze
2 cups heavy cream
1 lb. Belgian dark chocolate

¼ cup butter
Gold leaf from art store
To finish- ladle melted glaze over domes. Top with gold leaf accent. Return to fridge to hold and chill. It takes about 45 min in fridge to temper texture if using frozen.
This allows for easy preparation ahead for plating.

Serve with Crème Anglaise Custard
1½ cups milk
Vanilla bean or vanilla extract
3 egg yolks
2Tbsp. fine grain sugar

Method
Bring milk to a boil, with vanilla bean, remove after 5 min. (rinse bean well, and keep for further use).
Beat egg yolks with sugar until light and thick.
Whisk in hot milk, then return mixture to a low heat and stir constantly with a wooden spoon until mixture thickens slightly. Strain into a small bowl. Add extract (optional), keep in fridge.

58

Harleys

After leaving the big companies, I survived two years completely on my own; created my own business, did my custom tours, catered events and private dinner parties. All I thought about was business. The summer months ran into fall, fall into winter. I worked hard; all work and no play was not a good balance.

I had been single for eleven years and felt the weight of being alone. Vancouver had faded back into my first world. Would this be my lot? Where were all those sensible and darling men? I'd had dozens of unsuitable dates. Where to meet that special someone?

My angel intervened. "Look around, bring your head up into the light," she said. "I see a new love in your pathway."

Quite unexpectedly, a lady chef acquaintance from work knew someone recently divorced. She and I were on the phone.

Clara said, "My new live-in friend knows a guy who might be right for you." We continued to chat. "He might be too old for you though," she chuckled, (a little joke as both of us had always attracted much, much younger men). This man was eleven years my junior. She gave him my phone number.

After we set a date three times, he kept changing it because of conflicting business. I thought he was too flaky, ready to write him off.

He called again and said, "For sure I won't let you down, no matter what, I really want to meet you." I think now he saw it as a challenge.

He did sound sincere. We finally met for dinner at a prearranged restaurant in San Francisco near my house. Dinner wasn't extraordinary but conversation was easy. When he departed, I had a strange pinging feeling inside, as if my hormones were short circuiting. Hmm?

His name was Mike and he had a good sense of the world around him, used correct grammar, had lovely eyes, seemed into me from the start, and he was funny. My list of requirements had shifted over the years; think of the person under the façade my inner voice said. This time maybe he didn't need to wear a suit and tie all the time.

Mike said, "I had a great time, I'll call you soon."

You know, they all say things like that, so I brushed it aside and let it go. I don't remember much of the date but we parted on a good note. He seemed impressed. I wasn't ready to commit, played it cool. The next day I was surprised by a message on my answering machine from Mike.

"Hey, Barbara, can we get together over dinner in my neighborhood this time? There is a nice restaurant near here I want to take you to. I'll pick you up."

He lived across the Bay in Piedmont, a good area. Mike sounded excited and left his number in case I wanted to call back. We did connect and before too long we were getting together almost every week. I started to notice all the good things about him. Mike was in the commercial paint business and had had his own company before the divorce. He was about 5'9, eleven years younger, attractively dressed in a sport coat and chinos, nice shoes, (I did have a thing about shoes,) trim, courteous, cute, a great kisser, romantic and those twinkly eyes. I did go carefully though. If this worked into something, I had to be sure about what was below the surface. Was he trustworthy? Was he sincere when he murmured, "I love you?" What could he bring to the table, his love and maybe added financial support? I had gone through so much. Was I being too careful?

I had worked really hard to stabilize my life; create my career, acquire my fabulous house and my stylish silver Porsche! For a long time now it had been only about me. Did I want to share some of that? After all there are a lot of weird guys out there with lots of baggage.

When I met Mike, besides the initial sparks and the fun of a new romance, he had something else that attracted me. He was a rider; a motorcycle rider. He had been a rider almost all his life. Not the beer drinking, bar carousing type but one who rode for the thrill of speed when he was younger. Now the whiff of fresh cut hay or the aroma of orange blossoms in his face as he cruised along a country road was enough. He was a purist riding with no windshield, and no trendy showy clothes, I envisioned us riding off into the sunset.

I had never ridden before, had never tried. It would be a new thrill for me. If I could master this, it was something I could bring to the relationship. Mike was excited to think that we could be riders together and was impressed to think I would try. His former marriage had many things go wrong, but being pushed to sell his bike was the last straw for him. I felt riding could be a wonderful bond between us.

I said, "If we are going to think about riding, I it has to be a Harley." I wanted the 'bling' that was the Harley mystique.

Mike said, "If I had my way I would buy a BMW." So our ideas went back and forth and of course in the end we bought a Harley Sportster.

Now Mike agreed to go with me to take the Motorcycle Safety Course which consisted of three evenings of paper instruction and six

Saturday mornings of real riding under the control of two instructors. I was really nervous when the first morning dawned. It was cold and rainy but we carried on anyway. There were twenty five participants, mostly twenty-something guys, there to get their certificate leading to a legal license. I was the oldest of course, sixty-nine, and the only woman.

I figured it would be easy. My Porsche 911 had a stick shift, and I smoothly managed all the steep San Francisco hills. How hard could a motorcycle be with its gears and foot work? I was wrong. It was really a challenge but I was still determined.

The instructors wheeled out 25 Honda bikes, and positioned them on the tarmac. At first we all made a go at just wheeling the bike forward. Next we climbed on just walking it forward with our feet, and worked the gears, then turned on the key while in neutral. I was cold, wet and nervous. The engine growled and I shot forward out of control because I had rolled the throttle the wrong way. For motor-cycles, the throttle is rolled back, not forward as would be expected. This movement needed to become comfortable and automatic if I was going to continue. I was really scared. I had a live machine under me.

I said to myself, repeating, "Don't forget, you have a clutch and a brake; you can be in neutral any time."

That first morning at the safety course, at break time, I said to Mike, "I can't do this in the rain. I thought it would be easier." I could see he was disappointed but I was exhausted.

The instructor said, "If you drop out now, you will have to wait for the next session six weeks from now." He encouraged me to keep going.

The course was really tough, but not for Mike. He could have been one of the instructors. I continued with the course. On the last morning, I failed the crucial tight turns, I was depressed.

The instructor said, "When the next course begins, just come for the last morning when we do the final tests, and do it again, you know how to do everything else."

So that's what I did. I managed all the fast stops, plus the six cone slalom course with the tight angled turns in low gear. I passed it all. I drove home in my car, flushed with excitement. Mike was waiting for me out on the driveway to hear the results.

"I passed. I passed," I shouted, "Get out the Martinis." It was only 1.30 in the afternoon, but 5 o'clock somewhere. This was such a big accomplishment for me. Before too long we were laughing and having this wonderful celebration thinking about what might be ahead. By six PM and pretty tipsy, we turned out the lights and called it a day. I had taken a big step toward my future with Mike.

59
French Camp

My five summers in charge of creating inspired French Cuisine for La Maison Française, a program sponsored by University of California, at Berkeley, required a whirlwind of energy. All things French surrounded my waking hours and nightly dreams during the semesters from one year to the next.

'French Camp' as it was fondly referred to, offered a full immersion program for one-week in the heart of the California wine country at White Sulphur Springs, a resort minutes away from the town of St. Helena in the heart of Napa Valley. Quaint cottages for guests are dotted throughout the wooded grounds, creating a serene atmosphere. A central clubhouse holds a large kitchen and reception rooms. The program, offered for many years by the French Language Extension Program at Cal Berkeley was a way for students to experience France while remaining in the USA.

Topping out at forty lucky students, the program was widely successful among teachers wanting to upgrade their knowledge and worldly travelers of every persuasion preparing for their next trip to that part of Europe. It was an adult group.

The curriculum was aimed at participants of medium or better understanding of the French language, wanting to advance more than just their silent page knowledge. Written and speaking skills require so much more! To willingly assume the risks of speaking out loud in this foreign language took courage.

The opening reception included drinks and nibbles while introducing the professors, culinary staff and general routines. Right away the food team was in action. On Monday, the program got down to business after our hearty breakfast. Every day the group was paired off into small clusters of eight. Five language professors leading the groups were in charge of prompting spoken dialogue for about two hours each morning. Then all the groups changed rooms and another scenario was presented.

"Pretend you are in a seaside café. How would you speak to the *garcon*? Which way to the church or museum?" Professor Schwartzbart said. These were some of the queries. Then more complicated conversation between everyone spiraled at a faster pace, all in French. Everyone was supposed to speak only French the entire week, even in their social hours and by the pool.

He said, "Remember, This is *tout pour vous,* this is all for you. This is why you came!"

Seminars and French movies, (no sub titles), filled some of the afternoons, but there was also free time to schmooze with the other participants, lie in the sun by the pool to read and understand the next assignment, or build camaraderie amongst each other. However the segment of each day never to be missed was mealtime, breakfast, lunch and dinner! Everyone turned up for that. For many it was the high point of the day.

"What will be the tempting *surpris* today?" someone asked. Another voice, a doctor from Long Island said, "My friends gave me their list of the best restaurants in Napa but the best restaurant is right here in our own kitchen, I won't even go into town."

Each summer, many of the same students returned to experience the best time of their lives. This required me to create a new, fresh set of menus each year. Many hours of research and testing was necessary for perfect presentation, with side notes to remember all the quirks and ideas, uncovering the flavors typical of Provence, the coast or Le Loire. This was repeated three times a day for 40 guests. For six days. Exhausting! Sometimes the audience applauded their appreciation and shouted, "Bravo;" sometimes they were almost brought to tears by the changing table-scape of vines and blossoms and the beauty of the food. Wine at dinner also created lively conversation in French. Each day seemed to surpass the one before. By Friday we had built to a great crescendo as the final dessert of forty Hot Lemon Soufflés was presented to a standing and whistling ovation.

Each year I vowed it had to be my last, remembering the August heat, lack of air conditioning and the toll it took on my body. But like childbirth the pain faded and I agreed to take on yet another season.

'French Camp' paid well and a nice profit carried me forward into the fall/winter ahead. I was surviving.

I was into my third go-around doing this "thing" for the Berkeley professors. Mike, my new amour, was curious about this exalted and ambitious project in Napa. He had no idea what all the fuss was about.

I said, "When I drive to the valley preparing for the start of the event with all my extra equipment and big order of specialty foods, why don't you come in your car after work and see what we're doing? Maybe you could even help in the kitchen." By this time, Mike and I had been dating for several months and it was going quite well.

I had hired two prep people to assist and also to act as wait staff; also a chef friend from Albuquerque had flown to San Francisco to be part of my team. Jerry Wauqui was a full-blooded American Indian and knew his way around a restaurant. He was young, a big guy and full of energy.

Mike appeared in the kitchen just as we were plating up the entrées for that night.

He said, "What can I help with?" Jerry was at the big gas stove keeping forty duck breasts seared to pink perfection. I was dashing to the other stove to plate the vegetables and extras, checking the plate edges with a clean *serviette* for any wayward sauce, before being sent out the door. It all had to be perfection.

Jerry and I both shouted, "Just stay out of the way!" I'm sure that was just what Mike wanted to hear! Ha ha.

As the last table of six was served, I took a deep breath, turned around and hugged Mike letting him know I was so glad to see him.

That evening after the kitchen was clean and the next morning's breakfast set-up was ready to go, Mike and I walked hand in hand as dusk settled into the nearby wooded trails. On a whim, we took a skinny dip in a secluded, warm, mineral hot tub. The purple darkness of the forest allowed the sky to shower us with a velvet cloak of stars; imparting a romantic setting never to be forgotten.

Mike said, "I think we should get married. Will you marry me?"

I wanted to say yes, but....it was too soon! Was he too eager; "Let's talk about this when the job here is done and we're back in San Francisco." I didn't want any extra distractions, needing all my energy for the present event.

The next day the weather was so hot. The valley often reached triple digits. All the staff, were stressing out behind the hot stoves, peeling potatoes to make sautéed potato ovals. It was lunchtime, and plating up the first course of chilled Basil/Bisque with chive blossoms, I felt like I was having a heart attack or was suffering from heat stroke. I disappeared into the walk-in cooler and collapsed on a crate of asparagus.

Jerry called out, "Barbara, where are you?"

I opened the cooler and staggered out. I said, "I'm okay," but it gave everyone a scare, including myself.

About eleven that night when the swimming pool lights had been extinguished for the evening and all the guests had retired, all my staff including Mike and I decided to lay back and take a midnight swim. Someone said," Let's skinny-dip, the water is so silky, it feels delicious." We were feeling a little spacey after such a hot day.

I thought, "What a great idea, and promptly pulled of my suit, putting it on the edge of the pool." No sooner had I done that, the lights flashed on and I was right in the spot light. What could I do but swim over to recover my suit, stand up and put it on.
I was as nonchalant as I could be to the chorus of, "Go, Go, Go," like a strip club!

The next day, my kitchen staff was quiet, busy with their regular routine. No one mentioned the pool. It was so hot in the kitchen that I started to grumble again.

I said, "I'm burning up."

Someone said, "So take off your clothes"

I looked up with a raised eyebrow.

To make his point...with a sly smirk, he said, "It worked really well last night"

Everyone laughed. I was now known as the Wild Chef of Napa.

BOUDINA, SINGLE SERVING WARM MOLTEN CHOCOLATE CAKES

When I was doing my chef thing at French camp, I was producing these little cakes, turning out forty at a time. A useful recipe as the cakes can go to the oven from the freezer!
Molten chocolate mini cakes have become a restaurant rage.

Serves 12
12-3" metal rings 2 ½ high
Easy

1-⅛ lb. bitter/sweet chocolate
7/8 lb. un-salted butter
1½ cups sugar
9 eggs
1½ cups flour
1½ tsp. baking powder
1½ Tbsp. Bakers cocoa
12 Metal rings, parchment paper
Mascarpone or whipped cream optional
Mint leaves

Method
Sift flour, baking powder and cocoa. Set aside.
Set out rings on parchment lined baking sheet.
Chop chocolate and place in medium metal bowl over simmering water on stove.
Cut butter in small pieces and incorporate into chocolate.
Stir in sugar, then eggs one at a time.

The batter will be like brownie batter but a different ratio of chocolate. Fold in flour.
Drop batter or pipe into rings, ¾ full.
This will allow batter to expand when baking.
Freeze on sheet pan, then stack in freezer until needed.

When ready to bake, (allow ½ hour from baking to serving).
Bake in pre heated oven 400 (oven temp will come down to 375 because of frozen batter), until edges of cakes looks dry but center is still soft, about 10 minutes.
Remove to counter and let rest 5 minutes to set up, run a thin knife around inside of ring, let slide onto plate.
Serve with whipped cream dollop on side with extra cocoa dusted over. Add mint leaf.

60

The Two Bordelaise

Back, before I left Vancouver for San Francisco, Sid Cross, a good friend and a much admired wine expert, said, "If you join any culinary organization in San Francisco, the I.W.F.S, (International Wine and Food Society), Marin branch, is the one! Many of the important food people across the States are members." Thanking him, I tucked it away. While I was working hard at my new job, my off hours were spent equally earnestly pursuing new contacts in the Bay area. I followed up on my friend's advice and submitted my credentials for membership with the I.W.F.S. A few days later, I received my membership card welcoming me and they also included their monthly news-letter. Inserted in the travel section was a luxury program for one week in Bordeaux. Hmm. Read on.

The Two Bordelaise, Jean Pierre Moullé, the chef at Chez Panisse for the past twenty years, and Denise Moullé, his wife, wine connoisseur and representative for her father's fine French wines, were offering an insider's week in Bordeaux. Guests stay in a seventeenth century chateau turned bed and breakfast; cooking with Jean Pierre, expert wine tasting in the vines with Denise and eating oysters on the Atlantic coast in Acheron. Dinner at Château Bonnet, Denise's parents' palatial home and Jean Pierre and Denise's own gorgeous renovated barn in the village of Entre-Deux-Mers was included. Other destinations generally not available to the public, known only to the locals, plus dining at one and two star restaurants, sounded intriguing. The Wine Spectator Magazine had given the trip a glowing review. Could I afford it?

Anne said, "See if there is still space and then decide. It would fit your week of vacation perfectly." International calls to France set it all in place and I was ready to go.

"Yes, they could take one more in the group that would make eight, *mais oui.*" Jean Pierre said.

I still needed air fare, and almost like magic, a tiny ad for a charter to Paris was advertised in our city paper, leaving that Saturday and returning the following week. The price was so low I wondered if it was a scam. Maybe I had to bring my own food or pack water wings for the flight. But no, it was real. They were obviously trying to fill the last few seats. Only angels could account for all these happy coincidences.

I was getting braver at travelling alone; managing the ticket barriers at the train and metro, while heaving my luggage on to the next destination. At one information kiosk, I explained in broken French, how the turn-style had eaten my ticket but the agent just nodded and shrugged his shoulders. He threw up his hands in a French gesture exasperated at such a stupid tourist. After three such exchanges with me he just shoved a ticket towards me and went to the next person with a roll of his eyes.

The T.J.V. (as the fast train is known), from Paris was smooth and soundless, the farms and endless rolling hills of lush vines slipped past the windows. What would Bordeaux look like? I was excited at my tenacity to have managed this trip so far, I was a long way from home. I had arranged for pick-up at the front of the station. It had been a long day of travel. Already getting dusk, most of the travelers had hurried to their car or over to the nearby bus depot. I began to worry. Was I in the right place? I adjusted my sun hat and straightened my jacket one more time. I tried to look nonchalant.

Finally a likely car pulled over, it was my contact, Denise! She reached over and opened the passenger door, saying in a thick French accent mixed with English, she knew it was me because I looked so American in my hat.

Denise said, "I am so sorry to be late, I could not inform you ahead of time because the "Fan" was broken." What did that have to do with it?

It took me two miles and more French words to realize she meant the phone. I felt like Inspector Clouseau in the Pink Panther movie.

The bed and breakfast Château overwhelmed me. A mysterious, dark fortress, it was set back from the road with a meandering pebble driveway shrouded by trees, which brought us to a massive entry with stone statues and classic shrubs. Now on closer inspection, I could see lights twinkling in several high arched windows. They beckoned me inside, releasing my apprehension.

Our group came from all over the map; everyone was very foodie and wine travelled, bringing diversity and an unusual mix of backgrounds to the table. Jean Pierre was charming and very French as he demonstrated different foods and recipes at the professional kitchen at Château La Louvière or in his own rustic barn. His accent was musical and quite easy to understand. To catch Denise's words you had to use some imagination and watch her body language.

I said, "Watch out for the fan," and everyone laughed when I recounted my story about my poor French and Denise's broken phone.

The week was a glorious blur of food, wine and camaraderie. Expensive yes! But worth every penny.

Here is Jean Pierre's dessert recipe for Pear Clafoutis with Honey and my recipe for Caneles. Both recipes are very special to Bordeaux.

PEAR CLAFOUTIS WITH HONEY

This fragrant, summer, ripe pear dessert came from Jean Pierre when I was in Bordeaux as part of his special group hosted at his rustic barn in the Bordeaux countryside. A Sauterne or dessert wine would be a good pairing.

Easy

Tart Pastry, (Chez Panisse)
2 cups flour
½ cup sugar
½ cup unsalted butter
Pinch salt
1 egg yolk
1Tbsp. cold water
1 drop of vanilla extract

Filling
4 ripe pears
3½ Tbsp. fragrant honey
2 eggs
2 egg yolks
2Tbsp. sugar
2 oz. cornstarch
9 oz. half and half
1½ oz. sliced, toasted almonds

Method
In food processor, add flour, sugar, pinch salt and butter cut into small pieces.

Blend briefly.
Add egg yolk and water and vanilla.
Blend only to crumbly stage.
Wrap in plastic, chill for 1 hour.
Preheat oven to 400. Roll out pastry and line a 9" tart tin with removable bottom.
Chill again for 30 minutes.
Place tart shell on lower rack
And bake for 10-15 minutes until light brown.

Peel pears, remove cores and any seeds.
Cut each pear into eights.
In a non-stick pan, heat honey until foamy, then simmer pears for about 6 minutes, drain well.

Custard

Mix eggs and yolks with sugar and whisk until pale.
Add cornstarch. Add half and half.

Assembly

Place pears slices in concentric circles on pre baked shell. Add ¾ of custard and bake for 5-10 minutes.
Pour remaining liquid over fruit, add sliced almonds.
Bake for 20 minutes more until nicely browned.
Let sit to room temperature, dust with powdered sugar.
Cut in wedges.

LES CANELES

Another fascinating little French pastry was Bordeaux Caneles; batter poured into small, copper molds. The mixture bakes to a crisp outer finish due to bee's wax, yes melted bee's wax, coating the inside, and baked at a high temperature. It is very well known in the Bordeaux countryside. I brought the molds back in my luggage from Bordeaux. No worry then about airport security.

A Bordeaux regional specialty
About 30
Medium

4¼ cups milk
3Tbsp. unsalted butter
2 whole eggs
4 egg yolks
2¼ cups plus 3 tb. sugar
2 tsp. vanilla
2 cups plus 2 tb. unbleached flour
Wax beads, (available on the internet), or cooking spray.

Method
In a medium saucepan, bring 2 ½ cups milk plus the butter to a boil. Remove from heat.
In a large bowl, whisk together the remaining 1 ¾ of milk, sugar, eggs, yolks and vanilla.
In a steady stream, add milk/butter mixture.
Pass through a medium sieve.

Cover and refrigerate 24-48 hours.
Remove from fridge, and blend again.

Preheat oven to 400.
Place molds on a sheet pan. Melt wax and coat insides, or use cooking spray, but wax gives a better finish.
Pour batter into small, copper Canele molds to ⅛ from top.
Bake until cakes slip easily from mold and are well browned, about 1¼ hours.
Remove molds and enjoy dark and crisp pastries with a soft center.

61
The Beideman Street Group

When I was downsized out of my job, I was frantic. I'd had
this demanding position with ARA, (ARAMARK) for
two years and all was going well. When I bought my
house two years before, Paul said, "If you lose your job how will you
pay the mortgage?" Those haunting words!

I scoffed and said, "That won't happen." Now it had come true. I
immediately scoured the other food service companies for a similar
job, but as great as I felt I was, this position was the first to go. I could
transfer to their head office in Philadelphia but I had just purchased
my perfect home in San Francisco so I turned that down. It seemed
everyone was cutting back. I hadn't prepared for a slow economy.
I tried to be philosophical about my situation. Was there a positive
side to my dilemma? Maybe, but only if I dug down, I needed to take
a deep breath and move forward; be grateful for what I had accomplished so far.

Working for yourself has pros and cons. Follow the whispers of
your inner voice, then take the consequences or…have someone else
dictate how you spend each day (or night)! It would be would be

less pressure to just follow along, but is that what really spins your wheels? No.

Now I was able to wake up in my perfect house instead of a hotel room in another city: able to pace my day instead of pouring my guts into the corporate machine. How to earn a paycheck though? How can I keep my house? Challenged again! Will it ever end?

I culled through my many associates and acquaintances to test the waters for consulting or catering events. Cooking was still what I knew best. I sent out a brochure letting people know I could make their next party or wine festival the best yet. Just call me for a quote. My folder stated some important past clients: His Highness the Aga Khan, Charles Schwab, BC Hydro, Canada, Jaguar, Canada, the Australian ABC film crew, and numerous commercial or private events: plus of course my short bio on the back fold stating my training and experience and write-up by Bon Appétit Magazine.

The Beideman Street Group took shape; I was open to any format. Friends referred lots of business to me and I seemed okay.

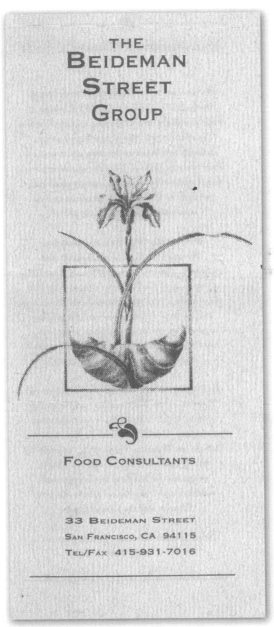

THE
BEIDEMAN
STREET
GROUP

—⁊⁊—

FOOD CONSULTANTS

33 BEIDEMAN STREET
SAN FRANCISCO, CA 94115
TEL/FAX 415-931-7016

My professional brochure for my new consulting company.

62

FunFrance Travels

Lying in bed, alone, I had a one-sided talk. "Don't be afraid to break out of the box." If I still want to travel, I will have to create my own destinations, niche markets, so different from what's available. With contacts in the wine industry, more ideas blossomed to invent my own boutique travel/tour company. I called it 'FunFrance Travels' and opened a web site. In order to offer such a tour, I had to go there and find all the special places that would interest my future clients. I wasn't just using the regular tourist program out of a book! What should I include? What would it look like?" Here is how I marketed my first tour;

* Château Drouilles Will Be Our Base,
The un-travelled Haute Vienne, Limousin Area of France.
*A Château of dreams. Complete luxury.
*All beverages, spa and relaxing massages included.
*Private mini bus, to wineries not usually available to the public.
*Cooking classes at 4 PM with Barbara in the
Grand kitchen at Château Drouilles.

`*Trips to Limoges, plus visit tiny village boulangeries,
and Foie Gras farms.
*Day trip to Cognac, custom tour with owner, Alan Royer
Special luncheon at one star restaurant
*An intimate group, only 12.
. **One price covers the entire trip, no add-ons. $3,500 per person**

Now was the time to go to France. The American dollar was favored seven-to- one. I set up a quick trip for myself so I could see these locations, securing all the logistics and meet with the important owners/managers in question. Even though I was thin on the French language, I managed. Everyone was very welcoming and looking forward to my group.

Back in San Francisco, I started to spread the word within all my food and wine contacts. One super contact was a local radio station in San Francisco that broadcast 'Food and Wine with Gene Burns,' every Saturday morning. The host took me under his wing and invited me as a celebrity guest chef on his weekend show. Everyone listens to Gene Burns, so as Gene and I talked up the trip and he raved on about the itinerary, the calls started coming in. We used up half an hour of air time discussing my elegant and different tour. He prompted me with many questions saying…

"Tell me about Château Drouilles? What will all this cost, how soon do people need to sign up, what was the phone number again?" allowing me to reiterate, giving dates and costs once more.

He said, "It sounds so fabulous I would like to go myself." This endorsement was all I needed to fill my French Adventure. My answering machine was filled with prospects when I returned from the show. It was magic.

Questions from prospective clients asked, "Are you sure there are no other hidden charges?"

"That's right; the fee includes everything, mini tours to wineries, food and even drinks. No unexpected charges at the end of the trip." I was taking a big chance.

This first custom trip was one week at Château Drouilles, near Blond in the Haute-Vienne province of Limousine, the center of France. The Château, a 16th century structure was a vision of twin towers nestled in an oak forest, the grazing sheep nearby made a bucolic scene. Besides the Château with its luxurious accommodations, there were quaint food and craft markets just three miles away. Guests could also go hiking in forested hillsides, or visit the nearby Limoges porcelain factory, to buy right from the source, so much to see!

Once everyone arrived in France and settled into Château Drouilles the fun began. The Château was so impressive. Tucked into the rolling hills, misty and magical, it was comprised of three levels of draped, twelve foot high windows, across the façade, with a sweeping circular approach to the welcoming front door. Everything was luxurious, from the modernized huge kitchen, cream velvet swags in the Hollywood dining room, to the exotic bedrooms, each with a huge down filled duvet quilt. My American guests just loved the unusual, quirky, European bathroom fixtures: bidets, and multi shower vents in the free standing shower.

Each evening I gave a cooking class in the fabulous Château kitchen, using fresh, local ingredients. After cocktails and nibbles in the salon, we listened to arias of live opera by one of my talented guests, beside the grand piano. Then we gathered in the "movie-set" dining room. Its' ten, tall windows draped in ivory velvet sheltered the guests at the expansive table which was set with candles, crystal goblets and flowers. Our dinner was the menu taken from the class, a splendid production each night. It sounds so easy, think of all the coordinating it took to assemble the right ingredients in a foreign country from a quaint market two hour's drive away. I was so exhausted once each evening's class was done, that I wondered why I had thought I could do it all! But it did come off perfectly, even my lesson using fresh Foie Gras.

Several more tours followed and each time Gene Burns welcomed me back on his show to tell his many listeners all about my next undiscovered destination.

DREAM WEEK

The Region...northwest of Limoges in the Haute Vienne province of Limousin.

The Château is a five-hour drive from Paris, or two hours by TJV train to Limoges or Angouleme, where car rental is available.

The Dordogne, Cognac, Armagnac and Bordeaux-centers for great wines, brandies, cheese and paté-are all within a short drive.

CHÂTEAU DROUILLES

*Château Drouilles, photo of chateau,
showing location and interesting description.*

My next tour to "Les Sources de Caudalie," an amazing new hotel and spa in the Bordeaux wine-country, was also a smashing success. The grown-up children of the famous family owned winery, Smith Haute Lafitte, were the creators of this wonderful destination. (Look up "Smith Haute LaFitte Winery and Spa" on Google). My Cognac contact from my last summer's travels, Alain Royer, gave me the inside scoop and introduction to this delightful family and destination. It's always who you know!

Gene Burns gave me more accolades while he interviewed me on his Saturday Wine and Food show. I was gaining access to the right people.

It was still the right time for US travel to Europe.

A little about Barbara

Barbara brings forth the flavor of life
as it is lived abroad.

Five summers as chef for U.C. Berkeley's intensive
residential French language program "La Maison
Francaise" in the Napa Valley of California, enriched
her passion for all things French and Mediterranean.

Cooking school owner and director of "Cuisine de
Barbara" for ten years in Vancouver, Canada
then merchandising specialist and corporate chef,
Barbara enjoys creating these custom wine and culinary
tours in France and Italy.

She resides at The Sea Ranch,
Sonoma County, California.

Our tour to Bordeaux 2000

TOURS 2001

Bordeaux • France
Tuscany • Italy

FUNFRANCE
TRAVELS...
and BEYOND

Barbara Miachika

Opera
Wine, Touring, Tasting
Cooking - Eating
Spa

For more information:
707/785.9536
BarbaraMiachika@funfrance.com
www.funfrance.com

Barbara's "FunFrance" brochure marketing her deluxe tour,
to Bordeaux, France. The photo shows her relaxed
in front of the famous Chateau Margeaux.

63
Mike

The pale San Francisco sun was sending shafts of filtered light through the sheer draperies hanging from the canopy around my bed. I reluctantly pushed back the cozy duvet and padded to the kitchen to whirl a blender drink, to fortify myself for the day.

In my little home office, notes and spreadsheets for a current project were all over my desk, waiting for me to compile them into a presentation for an afternoon meeting with a new client, the Oakland Ballet Society. If I could sell it with my presentation ideas, I'd be secure for a month. I needed to make it happen.

The president envisioned a huge dessert display for the premier evening performance of the Oakland Ballet's The Nutcracker Suite. The setting was to be in a retro theatre in that city. Someone on the committee had forwarded my name as the one to do the job. I was given *carte blanche* to prepare dozens of pastries. I chose Bavarian creams, chocolate and fruit fillings with many flavors to create all the desserts for 150 guests. The per-head allowance was $20. I could put into play some of my most interesting creations. The meeting was a huge success and the real work would follow.

My other contracts continued on. When doing a wine event, a private dinner party or heading up a tour, Mike was often there, so supportive and helping me when he was wasn't at work. He had a good food sense, could make a nice dinner or get the coffee going in the morning, but he was also Mr. Fix-It around the house. I relaxed and let it unfold and blossom. We laughed a lot. We fit well together. Before much longer I was ready to trust him. We talked again about our future. We were a couple.

Food was our common ground at the beginning. We had romantic evenings surrounded by candlelight while sipping pre-dinner cocktails. Oysters in a briny marinade made a delicious start. Delicate poached sea bass with basil, pungent Osso Bucco and creamy polenta, decadent desserts, some topped with whipped cream, all this created an irresistible scene. Brandies in warmed snifters followed us into the bedroom. At sixty- four I felt reborn.

PANNA COTTA WITH YOGURT

Try this wonderful dessert made with Greek yogurt.
It sets up in two hours, is the best thing to serve
after a heavy meal and guests will love it, trying
to guess what is so different in the mixture. It is of
course the Greek yogurt. This is a real keeper.
Serves 4,
Easy

1½ cups milk
1 envelope of plain gelatin
½ tsp. vanilla extract
1 cup heavy cream
¼ cup icing sugar
2 cups plain Greek yogurt

Raspberry coulis or other berry compote

Method

In a medium bowl, mix milk, gelatin and vanilla until gelatin
dissolves; set aside
In a small saucepan, combine heavy cream and sugar. Place
over medium heat and bring to a simmer.
Remove from heat and stir in gelatin mixture.
Transfer all to a bowl with a spout. Add yogurt and stir to
blend until smooth.
Fill 6 oz. ramekins and chill at least 2 hours or overnight. Serve
with fruit or plain.

My Third Life

64
A Place to Hang His Clothes

In the early 90's, the U.S. experienced a mild recession I described earlier, but by 1999 the pendulum had swung up again and housing in California was at a premium. Speaking with my children, still in Vancouver, they seemed unaware of the shifting economy coming their way. Canada was often six months behind. Maybe the earlier downward dip in the American market allowed the explosion of a new wave of business; nerdy dot-com companies, mainly in the electric hot bed of Silicon Valley, produced an astounding new breed of millionaire. Newly printed company stock immediately turned to cash in these investors' pockets. This phenomenon, the nouveau riche with their flush money, pushed housing prices to crazy heights. California real estate was on fire!

My darling Italianate flat in the center of San Francisco had turned out to be a precious jewel and I felt so lucky to have acquired it in 1992 while prices were still considered low. Out of my high end job for several years now, I scrambled every day to produce enough income to cover my expenses. I had chosen the right step down this lucky path, but could I keep going? Was my angel still watching over me to survive?

It was 1994 and Mike wanted us move in together but the arrangement of the rooms in my nest did not comfortably allow for an extra person without some interior construction. I was very bold to test his affection and his commitment to me. I was not planning to move from my house just to be with him.

My proposal said; "Create a second bathroom, with a closet for your clothes, and in the same space install a stacked washer/dryer." (Can you imagine I bought this place with no space for a washer?) The square footage was small, still it was a fabulous place, every room delightful, with high ceilings set off with original wood trim and a gas fired wood burning marble fireplace in the cozy front parlor.

Mike had the expertise and was willing to go the distance once we had worked out the floor plan. I said, "Take 5 feet from one of the rooms 7 ½ feet wide x 15 feet long, and using this back 5 feet create the desired extra room, enclosing an existing crawl space there for the stacked washer and dryer."

On week-ends, the lumber and tools arrived along with the help of one of Mike's friends. Permits were acquired and the plan went forward. It was all very exciting. My project was to select the bathroom décor, plumbing, lighting and laundry appliances. While the renovation progressed, five wooden stairs to the back garden were also repaired to perfect sturdiness. Altogether the resulting work was a huge improvement. There was now a second bathroom with a glamorous free standing porcelain basin with gold faucets all reflected in a mirrored back wall, black and white tiled floor and a closet for his clothes! The washer/dryer hid behind louvered doors. The house was now truly perfect! Mike moved in. We talked about marriage and our newly renovated home. When I secured a new house loan at a lower rate, I included Mike's name as part owner. This was the seal of my trust! We continued on.

65
The Century Club

I fell into an interesting job through an acquaintance, my next-door neighbor. The Century Club of San Francisco, the oldest private women's club in the city, needed a new chef and my resume was put forward. The club was conveniently located six blocks from my house. The kitchen was old, but workable. (The club really was one hundred years old.) It was up to me to prepare luncheon for a mid-week gathering of 100 ladies of social background, every Wednesday, right at noon. I had one prep helper and eight professional wait staff for plated presentation. For three years I enjoyed the rhythm and paycheck this provided and was also able to use the kitchen and wholesale food access for my own occasional catering, making each endeavor worthwhile. This was the last structured position of my career before Mike and I planned to marry in 1997. Together we would chart our new future.

66

Married in Vancouver

My boys and their wives were thrilled that I wanted to remarry. They readily welcomed Mike and, after some hopeful suggestions from me, Anthony and Victoria eagerly orchestrated a garden wedding to take place in their beautiful West Vancouver home overlooking Vancouver's harbor and the Pacific Ocean.

What a thrill for me to have my oldest son escort me through waiting family and guests towards the quaint arbor in the garden. This marked my new life. It was a catered affair with thirty-six of my close friends, and a few of Mike's, some of whom had flown to Vancouver from various parts of the country to wish us both well. This was a solid start and we could hardly believe our good fortune. Standing under a twig archway that Anthony had built just that morning using driftwood off their beach and vines from their garden, we said our vows in their lush hillside garden with the waves of the Pacific Ocean as a backdrop. After many toasts and cocktails, a delicious dinner was served on draped round tables set out on the patio giving everyone a chance to eat, drink and bless us with their presence. Candles and mini lights created the scene.

The caterers had been gracious to allow me to instruct their chef how to finish and present the Salmon Roulade appetizer, which I had assembled earlier in the day.

My touch was in almost everything; from my filmy, chiffon wedding dress of my own design, created many weeks before in San Francisco, to an unusual headpiece of papery white hydrangeas clustered atop a flowing veil, billowing around my head and shoulders. The veil was scattered with rosebuds giving it interest and a boutique quality. It was my chance to shine. Of course I baked the centerpiece white Chocolate Buttercream Wedding cake in the kitchen at a friend of Victoria's just down the hill.

Dancing to live music from a small quartet on the lawn, the party flowed into the night. My children had helped us put our best foot forward.

Our second ceremony held in our flower garden back home in San Francisco for those who missed the big day in Vancouver, was a reason to celebrate again. I did all the reception this time, and chose a dark chocolate Ganache over a white cake with sugared almonds as the special finish. I wore my wedding dress again, and the cloudlike head-piece of paper flowers. Mike was handsome in his flattering tuxedo with his color- coordinated floral bow tie.

SALMON ROULADE/COULIS AND CONFETTI OF VEGETABLES

More difficult
Serves 6
Enlarge recipe as needed.

Filling for salmon
2 leeks, white part only cut into a chiffonade
1 Tbsp. butter
Salmon
3 lb. center cut fillet, trimmed
Kosher salt, fresh cracked black pepper
Parchment paper

Method
Cut salmon open like a book, gently pound under plastic to an even thickness.
Sprinkle cooked leaks over. Add a touch of salt and a pinch of pepper.
Using parchment, create a tight roll, twist ends. Refrigerate several hours to set shape.
Spread aluminum foil. Paint with olive oil, dust with cracked pepper.
Remove salmon from parchment and tightly roll in foil, twist ends closed.

Fresh Tomato/Cucumber Coulis.
Drop tomatoes into processor, whirl, and strain juices.
Do the same with pieces of unpeeled English cucumber.
Whisk in good mayonnaise, thinning with mineral water to correct texture.
Taste for seasoning. Hold

341

Garnish of fresh vegetables

Cut grilled red pepper, fresh cucumber and plum tomatoes into even dice and shape.

Toss in bowl with cut chives.

Cooking salmon

Heat a large sauté pan, add peanut oil to film bottom.

Lay foil wrapped salmon log in hot pan, turn and roll to cook for about 4 minutes.

test done-ness by pressing foil for some resistance.

Remove and let come to room temperature, <u>about 1 hour.</u>

Assembly

Taste sauce for flavor, cut rounds of salmon (3/4") thick right through the foil. Remove ring of foil, place salmon onto each plate, spoon coulis around, sprinkle with diced vegetables.

Chef note, as you can see, this recipe is good to make ahead, perfect for catering and presentation. All the work is done ahead.

CEVICHE, SEAFOOD APPETIZER

I included Ceviche in my wedding buffet for our San Francisco friends. It tasted very fresh and cool for a warm outdoor event.

Serves 30
Easy

2 lb. sole, cod, snapper (mixed)
½ cup fresh lime juice
2 large white onions, thinly sliced
5 tomatoes, blanched, skinned, seeded, sliced
2 carrots, shredded
1 tsp. Oregano
4 Tbsp. minced parsley
3 Tbsp. fruity olive oil
Dash hot pepper flakes
S/P to taste

Cocktail breads or crackers

Method
Cut fish into 1" pieces and marinate in lime juice in stainless or glass bowl for 1 hour.
Toss. Add rest of ingredients <u>except</u> cilantro and marinate 1 more hour.

Add 2 bunches of Cilantro, finely minced and serve with crackers or toasted flat bread pieces.

*Barbara and Mike looking picture perfect
on their Wedding Day in West Van.*

67

The Sea Ranch

Mike had lost his paint business after the questionable dividing of funds following his quite recent divorce. Over and over he mused, "How could I have ended up so badly." He now hated working for someone else, everyday coming home unhappy and stressed. He was used to being in charge. I was used to doing my own thing too. We searched for all possible ways to put ourselves into this direction.

Our little flat was a golden nugget right under us. The housing market in 2000 was producing crazy prices. Agents were getting four and five offers on every listing. There was a buying frenzy. We decided to test the market. Because our house had two bathrooms, a cobbled and gated driveway, off-street parking and a renovated kitchen with a new stainless Viking stove and fridge, our agent immediately suggested $550,000.00 as a list price. We were astounded. One half a million dollars for 950 square feet! If it sold, our idea was to move up the California coast and find a house in need. We could do it! We were creating our new life.

I could feel the years telling me that the food business was now too tough on my bones. This idea of house renovation with Mike came at the right moment. The recent construction in our San Francisco home played out this scene. Together we said, "Buy one house at a time, live there for two years while improving it, reaping the capital gain by selling it for a profit." The landfall of cash from the sale of our perfect flat created the first needed nest egg to proceed. After that each finished house would provide for the next.

My glamorous life in San Francisco had come full circle, now I needed to look forward to new adventures with Mike, the love of my life

Searching for our next house needing repair brought us one hundred miles up the California coast. We found the perfect prospect in The Sea Ranch, a rugged area of northern California. The Sea Ranch was so unusual that it was written up in architectural journals as part of the curriculum for aspiring design students. It featured houses with a weathered, grey finish, tucked into the hardy landscape of the northern California coast. It was perhaps one of the first "green" experiments into new building codes.

Everything there was geared toward saving the environment. There were no street lights to spoil the twinkling evening sky. Mandatory recycling of trash, was the norm, and of course there was a wonderful community garden, three acres, called "Posh Squash." Members, at seventy-five dollars a year, were required to do just one morning of weeding a week from planting to harvest, to reap the benefits. The reward was unlimited picking of fruits and vegetables, as they came ripe. I loved the aromatic scent of fresh Arugula when cut from the earth. Some people joined just for the endless crop of raspberries; the berries so plump and juicy, the weight bending the branches. You could sometimes fill a basket from just one bush.

I joined Posh Squash, the tennis group and we played Petanque, a French game like Bocce. We both rode motorcycles and were part of the Retreads; an over-fifty group of hardy riders: all this while planning the renovation of our new house.

In the nearby town of Gualala, ten miles up the coast from The Sea Ranch, our nearest town, the community center was a gathering place for the arts and crafts as well as sporting activities. Like many small towns, people were drawn together here for friendship and daily activities. One such event was a planned dinner for about eighty people, headed up by a different steering group each month. One month Italian, another German or French. It was all supported by volunteers and several meetings always happened before the final menu was decided. This month was French. In town, people knew I was a pastry chef, so of course that was my category. The day before the dinner, I gathered all my ingredients for a special lemon cake and set to work. This was a cake constructed with several parts. Eight cakes would be needed, (each cake would give ten slices), and everything had to be expanded from the original recipe. I was able to borrow several spring form pans from the other members to make up the right number.

GATEAU ELEGANT AU CITRON

Why did I choose this cake? It was a show off Gateau, the flavor mellows as it sits and it cuts perfectly after refrigerating so no last minute worries. For me it was a chance to share a favorite recipe. Note the potato flour. I did it X 8.

Pre-heat oven.
Bake, 350 for 15 minutes, then 400 for 20 minutes.
10" spring form pan
Serves 10
Medium

Nut Biscuit Cake
7 eggs, separated
Pinch of salt
1 cup sugar
½ cup flour
⅓ cup potato flour
3 oz. almonds, pulverized
Zest of 3 lemons

Lemon Cream, 2 parts
½ can of sweetened condensed milk
⅓ cup fresh lemon juice
1 cup whipping cream, whipped

Part 2 Lemon Curd
7 yolks from above
¾ cup sugar
5 7/8 oz. unsalted butter

⅓ cup fresh lemon juice
⅓ cup dark rum, Myers
Zest of 1 lemon

Pistachio nuts, roasted, chopped

Method Cake
Place buttered parchment in bottom of 10" spring form pan.
Beat whites with pinch of salt, Carefully sprinkle sugar over to make a firm shiny meringue.
Sift flours, gently fold in then add pulverized almonds and zest.
Turn it into the pan.
Bake as above. Cool on rack.

Lemon Mousse
Blend condensed milk and juice in medium bowl.
Whisk heavy cream, fold into lemon/sweetened milk mixture.
Set aside

Method Lemon Curd
Make lemon cream while cake cools.
Place yolks, sugar, butter and lemon juice in a heavy bottomed saucepan.
Whisk over low heat until thickened, (coats the back of a spoon.)
Do not boil. Turn into small bowl over ice. Set aside.

<u>Assembly</u>

Slice cake horizontally into 3 thin layers.
Ponge cut surfaces with rum.
Place on cake board.
Fill layers with lemon/sweetened milk/cream mousse..
Cover outside with thin layer of same. Chill.
Use the lemon curd to over-ice top and sides giving a nice finish

Top off edges with chopped pistachios.

Serve with Raspberry coulis,(optional)

The dinner turned out perfectly. Everyone did their part for the other dishes and the whole event was a huge success. It would be another set of volunteers next month.

Our fixer-upper we had managed to buy in The Sea Ranch was in need of major changes. We could see the possibilities, it had good bones. So we started in! Reconfiguring the floor plan and long days of hard of physical work by Mike had proved worth-while. Inserting a large structural beam to support the overhanging second level to allow a complete new kitchen below was one of our best challenges.

Mike said to me, "When we looked at the idea of an improved main floor, taking away the existing load-bearing struts seemed impossible at first. There had to be a way to support the second floor without those posts." Consulting a structural engineer/architect was really worth the price of five hundred dollars for his advice. Without the right formula, we would always worry if the beam was strong enough.

When the huge laminated beam was delivered to our driveway, we felt we were building the pyramids. Mike coolly took me aside and said, "Let me figure out how this is going to be lifted into place with-out hiring big equipment that we can't afford." I had no idea about such things. It took two strong men. Mike and his friend Amir used only their arms to carefully lift one end, one inch at one end, then one inch at the opposite end placing the beam carefully on the end-pins. The overhead beam was put in place. It finally stretched across the twenty foot opening, resting on its end-pins. It was finally the right height. It was slow work but with two guys moving it together, it was possible.

I said, "Look what a fabulous room we have now!" When Mike laid down the Pergo wood flooring, the place just glowed. We continued to have these positive affirmations to each other as each new improvement emerged. All the main floor rooms were able to flow, one into the other. There were so many improvements that the original house was now swallowed up by these delightful new images inside and out.

Adding wall-mounted leaded glass cabinets over a sideboard in the dining room created decorative punch. Looking over to the stainless Viking gas stove and free-hanging hood, it shouted money and value for future buyers. Finally the addition of a revised front entry, now with double doors plus sweeping, rustic landscaping completed the look. We even had a Bocce court marked out on sixty feet of lawn with the colored balls for pitching. Our house had tons of curb appeal.

This work was not physically as hard on me as catering but produced lots of uncertainties and stress. Living in such a mess also takes perseverance. Mike did all of the carpentry with his friend arriving on the weekends to add an extra hand. I supplied mounds of nourishing food to revive us all each day, and was the runner for new parts, major appliances and another box of nails. Working side by side ingested a new depth of romance into our relationship. I loved this house, how it made me feel, and its connection to the earth. We were learning on the job! The renovation was going along quite well.

One evening after dinner, sitting out on the deck enjoying a coffee, I said, "I think we should get a dog. It would be one of the perks for choosing this rustic life style of wind-swept beaches and woody trails. It's a perfect place for a dog!" I had a picture in my mind of something shaggy, like a Wheaton or a Beardie.

All the time I was in San Francisco I promised myself if I moved to the country, I would get a dog. Until then, Alex, my stone guard dog on the front step, would have to do.

Mike wasn't open to the idea. I was surprised and disappointed, our first real fight, (discussion.) I thought he was just kidding me, but no, he was serious.

He said, "I've never had a dog, they tie you down and I won't pick up the poop, end of story."

I kept on, saying, "I will do all the work, and pick up the poop." Mike was very resolute and definite.

"What about when we ride?"

"I know a good pet sitter right here in The Sea Ranch. It won't tie us down too much." The rest of the evening was strained, noticeably tense.

I needn't have worried; the perfect dog was waiting for us in the Cosmos. Some may say its coincidence, chance or fate, but our darling Muffin's face had just been posted on a rescue site. He was part Wheaton and maybe part poodle or something. Not too small, not too big, just right. The vet said Muffin was maybe a year and a half old; he was house trained, mellow and grateful. The pound had picked him up on a street in Southern California, not too far from my sister's house in San Clemente. He was a little matted but so sweet. It is so hard to think of someone dumping him out like garbage. He had those wonderful eyes. We were already going south for Thanksgiving at my sister's house and his foster location was on the way. I think it was fate. We made a stop to see him. It all just fell together. In spite of Mike's reluctance, we arranged to adopt Muffin.

Before too long, Mike said, "What did we do before we had Muffin, our adorable furry child?" We were now three.

68

Annapolis Winery

While Mike was converting our fixer-upper into a beautiful home, I still drifted into dreams of escargot, pasta and pastries. It was impossible to leave my food life behind. The eclectic owners of a nearby hillside winery, an intriguing couple, Barbara and Basil Scalabrini, liked my suggestion to put on an exclusive dinner event in their cluttered cask room.

"But there is no space," they said at first. The Annapolis Winery, a small family affair nestled in an old orchard of apple and pear trees high on a hill looking out to the ocean, contained only a narrow tasting room up front for guests to sample the wines. In the warehouse, the working space, not open to the public, I envisioned dozens of candles, bunches of white Cyclamen planted in moist green moss centered down the long draped table to accommodate twenty special guests. White mini lights could wind through the foliage creating a magical setting. High above the long draped table, a chandelier filled with more candles would float like an illusion. Existing wine-filled casks, stacked to the sides with more candles on top, completed the vision. So I went ahead and planned the party. The evening arrived.

One of the guests said, "This is amazing, it feels like a movie set." At seventy-five dollars a person, the food itself had to be so perfect, and it was!

The Menu
Timbale of Earthy Mushroom Custards
with a
Truffle Sauce

•

Wild Pacific Salmon, Grilled, Ginger Glaze
Onion/Carrot and Fennel Marmalade

•

Coeur à la Crème
Posh Squash Raspberries.

•

Imported Cheese Plate and fresh Annapolis Grapes.

•

Wines from Basil's special reserve production complimented all the flavors. Many cases of wine were sold that night after the dinner. The Scalabrini's were so pleased and immediately saw the possibilities for more events. But one big production here and there was my limit now. Someone else could take over.

———————— ❧ ————————

CUSTARD TIMBALE OF MUSHROOMS WITH DEMI-GLACE TRUFFLE SAUCE

This was the starter for my special dinner party in the winery. These little oval, metal molds from France, (order on line), are the key to this success, they create a beautiful shape and are a perfect height. 3x2½.
At one time during my catering career I had 150 of these molds.

Serves 16
Oven 375, 35 minutes for small molds
Medium

¼ cup butter
⅔ cup shallots chopped
2 cloves garlic minced
1½ lbs. domestic mushrooms sliced
2 tsp. sea salt
1 tsp black pepper
6 eggs
2 egg yolks
1 qt. heavy cream
16, ½ cup molds, lightly buttered

Sauce
Demi-glace mix (Knorr brand) or from scratch.as follows.
Mushroom paste, and vegetable broth and liquid from dried
Cepes, mushrooms

Beurre manie, to thicken texture
Butter, brandy, lime juice
¾ cup chanterelle mushrooms sautéed, added to sauce for plate garnish

Method
Sauté sliced mushrooms in butter, shallots and garlic; cover and cook on medium to evaporate liquid from mushrooms.
Process this mixture on/off in food processor until smooth.
Add rest of ingredients and whirl on/off.
Fill molds, place all in water bath, bake on middle rack in oven about 40 minutes.
Let rest for 5 minutes, Loosen with thin knife to un-mold onto individual plates.
Have pre made demi-glace sauce, hot, or pre-fab, your own, as above. Finish sauce with swirl of butter, brandy and lime juice to taste.
Add touch of chanterelle mushroom pieces as garnish.

Ps. this is an impressive first course great for a dinner party. Molds and sauce can be prepared ahead and carefully re warmed in molds ready to plate up.

I was thinning bunches of baby carrots at Posh Squash one morning putting in my required one half day a week effort, and chatting with a woman I had just met, Lita Ghit. She was weeding in the next row. In her conversation, she mentioned North Vancouver and Ghit Pools, a swimming pool company her husband had owned there.

I gasped, "We used your company when our West Vancouver pool was enlarged. I remember the name." Here we were on our knees in a vegetable patch hidden from the world, sheltered from the wind-blown trees in The Sea Ranch. Wow, an instant flash-back to my first life set me back on my heels! We are all connected somehow. So amazing!

Mike said, "I think it's time to sell the house." The Sea Ranch area and surrounding inlets could feel the effect of the crazy San Francisco market prices that were still shooting upward but how long would it last, had we guessed right? We paced nervously each day hoping for a buyer. Finally, just before Christmas we had a solid offer. We were able to realize a sizable profit: we were in the money again.

Mike spun me around with a big hug and said, "We must have a champagne toast. Christmas will be better than we thought." Before the sale, our bank account was down to two hundred fifty dollars. This was cutting it way too fine.

We had created an interesting life style. If you have to always feel secure, this is not the direction for you. Two years had ticked by as we enjoyed this intriguing community. Our lives in The Sea Ranch mingled with the locals, but floated away two years later when we sold our house and moved on.

69

Cakes in Florence

We looked to the upper coastline, past Mendocino and into Oregon. Too much farther north meant the weather would be cold in the winter, so we concentrated on the southern area of Oregon and found Florence, a quaint town right on Highway One on the Pacific ocean.

Situated at the mouth of the Siuslaw River, Florence's "Old Town" was a collection of boutique stores and hardy restaurants. Spread out from there, mostly on the north side of the river, a decent population of nine thousand included two major groceries, a good community center, the usual fast food places and a lumber yard. Upon closer inspection, many smaller enterprises and realtors filled in the gaps. We picked Safe Harbor Realty, the only realtor who had bothered to answer our earlier queries to relocate and we went to work. With money in our pockets from the last renovation, locating a new place to live was all a big adventure.

Houses here were even more affordable than The Sea Ranch. While we surveyed the market, we lucked into a fabulous condo to rent for ourselves. Right on the river and beside Old Town, in the heart of everything, it was an instant decision and we made that our base of operations. Our plan of one house renovation at a time was working very well. This time we didn't live in the mess. Surrounded by success from earlier deals we were allowing ourselves to think we had the perfect arrangement. For a time we did. We bought and sold three houses in Florence. Mike was kept busy and I was soon to be too!

Out riding one weekend with new biker friends, Steve and Karen, Steve mentioned a special bakery, listed on the market right in town. The listing was very appealing because it was filled with tons of equipment. Steve knew it would be tantalizing to me, hard to resist.

I said, "I've done enough of that and I'm really not interested. Most of my pans and equipment have been given away because I am ready to retire." We rode some more and when we stopped for lunch, he mentioned it again.

He said, "I have the key and could show it to you," a clever agent.

Cakes were still my passion, so when this fully set-up wholesale space appeared, I was blown away. The previous owner had succumbed to cancer, leaving everything intact; there was still flour and sugar in the big bins, and eggs stacked in the reach-in. Again it seemed like fate. Of course I said, "I'm buying this place." Mike was there but I didn't even consult him. I was so sure!

It was fun for a year and a half. Business was brisk and we supplied scones, pastries and petite cakes of various kinds, every-day to the local latté shop. I soon taught Mike how to make the scones, so he ended up having to be at the shop at 6 AM with me. Anything we baked, they eagerly bought. At a quaint lunch/dinner restaurant in Old Town, called the Depot, I supplied a mile high chocolate cake so delicious, that customers reserved cake with their dinner reservation. Some weeks I delivered as many as fourteen cakes. My bulk orders for cases of butter, sacks of flour and cartons of buttermilk became common-place.

Private parties and special events filled my days. I revived my Cuisine de Barbara name and even held cooking classes in the evenings. Wedding cakes were a big money maker but stressful. To stay ahead of my competition, I perfected "Rolled Fondant" to finish many of the wedding cakes. This was a revival of the old English style, but now a silky thin coating as different as night and day from the original. There was a woman in Harrisburg, Pennsylvania that was expert at doing this Fondant in this different and modern way. Calling her for more information regarding her classes, I was energized to join her next series at her school. Airline tickets and hotel reservations in my pocket, off I went for one week to acquire the technique for perfect Rolled Fondant. As I look at the current cake extravaganzas on television, I still don't see the artists using this unique method? Maybe they aren't aware of it.

One of my silky, flourless chocolate cakes was now a star at a small breakfast/lunch/ tea room in the Old Town district. I sold it only to her. The owner had an eclectic décor within her restaurant that was different and so appealing, a New York touch.

CHOCOLATE CLOUD CAKE IN A FOREST

Each small mouthful is very smooth and dense, a play on silk pie. High chocolate rolls like cigars on end encase the perimeter and stand like a fortress around the edges, very dramatic and so perfect for her Tea Room.

9" spring form pan
Advanced

Make ahead, one 8" chocolate layer cake, ¾ inch thick.

Filling
1½ cups heavy cream
1 cup sugar
2 cups dark cocoa powder
1 stick unsalted butter, (½ cup)
3 cups heavy cream, lightly whipped
Orange liqueur, (I like Grand Marnier) for cake surface,
Raspberries and 1 lb. of dark, semi-sweet chocolate for cigar curls.

Method
In a saucepan heat cream and sugar, bring to a low simmer, remove from heat and whisk in cocoa and butter until smooth, cool.
Fold in whipped cream.
Line a 9" spring form pan bottom with parchment.
Place 8" cake layer in bottom, sprinkle with liqueur.
Pour chocolate mixture into pan, over cake, covering cake filling pan to top.

Smooth surface and chill, several hours or over-night.
Unmold on to a cake board, just 2" bigger than pan. This
allows for final cake decoration around the outside.
The extra mousse filling around the 8"cake in the pan helps
the curls to affix securely.

Melt the chocolate in a stainless bowl over simmering water.
Stir to smooth. Let cool slightly (See back index, working with
chocolate)
Spread on the back of a sheet pan as for creating small or
large cigar shaped curls.

I met with wedding cake clients in the cosy front area of my shop to discuss their cake requirements. I had all the walls draped with off-white canvas, creating the image of a French Boulangerie. I thought it was très chic.. Sometimes brides would call from far away as New York or Chicago to plan their cake. Rolled fondant was in vogue and I felt confident now, working with it after my intense workshop with Julie Bayshore, the expert in Harrisburg, PA. I was busier than I had ever anticipated.

Wedding Cake covered with meringue hydrangeas from my bakery. Cuisine de Barbara, Wedding Cakes, custom pastries, now situated in Florence Oregon.

Here is the famous scone recipe that Mike turned out every morning while I mixed bran muffins. We worked side by side, all the ovens were on and baking at six thirty A.M.

Mike's Corn Meal Scones with Blueberries

Makes 40
Oven 375
20-25 minutes

Easy

10½ cups flour
6¼ cups cornmeal
2¼ cups sugar
6Tbsp. baking powder
3 tsp. salt
1¾ cups chilled unsalted butter
2Tbsp. lemon zest
4 cups dry blueberries
6 cups low fat buttermilk
1½ tsp. vanilla

Method

Combine dry ingredients in a large bowl. Add lemon zest.
Cut in butter.
Combine buttermilk and vanilla, adding to dry ingredients last, with hands, just pressing together.
Divide dough into 2 large portions.
Turn out on the counter, divide again each portion into 2 = 4 pieces.
Roll and press into discs ½' thick.

Add dry blueberries over bottom half, press disc on top,
patting edges slightly.
Place on sprayed sheet pan.
Egg wash top, cut into wedges like pie, don't make too big as
they expand in baking.
Bake on middle rack.

Chef tip, placing blueberries on dough, not mixing directly
into all the batter keeps dough cleaner.
If using currants or raisins, mix directly into batter.

DRIED CRANBERRY/ORANGE MUFFINS

These muffins were popular at the local latté shop. Some days I added a different flavor of muffin but still had the Blueberry ones. Blueberry is the overall favorite. The shop bought them all.

Easy

Yield 36
Oven 375-400, 25 minutes

4½ cups flour
2¼ cups sugar
6 tsp. baking powder
1 tsp. salt
1½ cups non-fat liquid milk
¾ cup vegetable oil
3 tsp. orange zest
¼ cup diced fresh orange
3 eggs, lightly beaten
3 cups dried cranberries, plumped in hot water, drained.

Method
Preheat oven.
Combine dry ingredients in large bowl.
Combine milk, oil and zest, add to center of bowl.
Stir with wooden spoon, add cranberries.
Spray muffin tins, fill ⅔ full.
Bake in 400 on middle rack. (See note re temperature above.)

70
Florida

One of Mike's brothers had a vacation house in Cape Coral, Florida. (Did I ever mention Mike was one of thirteen children?)

Tom said, "Come and visit Marylou and me during the winter season when the Florida weather in January consists of sun and warm breezes."

Mike said to me, "Maybe Florida would be a good place to retire. We could buy a fixer-upper, sell it and then find a forever house."

I had visions of maybe living on a power boat.

Mike said, "If we lived on a boat we might bump into Jimmy Buffet." We both laughed and daydreamed. He said, "You are working way too hard at this baking thing. You must try to sell the bakery."

We worked on our new idea for six months trying to decide how to proceed. In August, Mike flew out to Florida to work on our plan. He met with his brother and a local property agent and selected a house needing our touch. When he returned to Oregon I had good news for him. I said, "I've sold the bakery for a small profit, (not great but it is all cash,) so we now have that money to add towards the move. We are free to go." I knew it was time to leave the baking life-style behind me.

Driving across the country to our next house with a pick-up truck full of tools and just some of our belongings, we felt like the Clampets from Beverley Hills.

71

Cape Coral

We did a fabulous job on the Cape Coral house. We lived in the mess for six months instead of paying rent in a motel. We were being practical. Our plan had seemed so secure. We were busy doing our own little thing, transforming the house from old and dingy to up-dated and inviting.

I think you can guess what's coming. The economy was starting to combust and we didn't see it. We were caught up in the recession of the century. Worry and soul searching engulfed our days while we decided what to do. Every day the house was worth less. The housing market continued to fall. We lowered the price. Then lowered it again but still no buyers! To mark time while we waited hopefully for a sale, we started taking day trips to other parts of Florida to see what could be next. Where should we be?

Mike said, "The warm sunshine is still so appealing, we should try to stay in Florida." I agreed.

72
Tanglewood

A full page advert for Tanglewood caught my eye in Cape Coral's Sunday paper. An over -fifty -five 'park' in Sebring, central Florida, boasted relaxed living in a special community offering endless amenities and a fun lifestyle. I didn't know anything about 'parks', but was soon to find out.

It was a beautiful place, great landscaping, big pool, shuffleboard, horseshoes, pool tables, Pickle-Ball, tennis courts and a big clubhouse. What is Pickle-Ball? Was this for us? We both loved the idea of a fresh start. The last few lots in Tanglewood were filled with new homes. It was quite a big complex, twelve hundred homes. The model we liked had a big kitchen with a movable center island, two bedrooms, two bathrooms, a cozy den, a big living/dining space and a screened lanai. A brand new house; this was appealing after living in dust and plaster for six months.

This community offered a lot for the money. We felt we could afford a house here. The prices seemed low, so we applied for a bank loan right there and then in Sebring. We were approved. This was still the land of easy money.

After eight months, our poor investment in Cape Coral was finally sold off at a huge loss. Real estate had been a good money maker for us before, but now we had to adjust to this financial set-back. All over the country people were caught short with this recession. All our hard work had been for nothing. We looked at every possibility to avoid bankruptcy, but there was no other solution. The only bright light here was, we had already purchased the Sebring home. It was to be our primary residence so it would be exempt from the cloud of bankruptcy.

Our lawyer pointed out, "Your only income apart from house renovation has been Social Security. Neither one of you are in the daily job market now. You have used up your entire cushion. You cannot pay off this huge debt you have incurred while waiting to get a buyer. Bankruptcy will allow you to go forward." It was a bitter pill to swallow. We had always had excellent credit before!

On the phone to my kids I said, "We've bought a place in Tanglewood, a trailer with upgrades!" The nicer terminology was a 'Manufactured Home.'

There was dead air over the phone, then Anthony said, "Are you sure this is a good thing." He was trying not to judge too quickly. He had never heard of the place. I'm sure he imagined the worst; tumbledown shabby trailers in a poor neighborhood. More conversation, then details on the internet painted a better picture for him. We invited all the kids to come for a visit to see where their mother had landed.

After their visit, they said, "Tanglewood is a fabulous place, and your home is amazing, not like a trailer at all, this could work."

Victoria, my daughter-in-law said, "Mom, wherever you are, you have always created a beautiful home." They endorsed our choice. They were glad we had found our footing.

I had wistfully given up the idea of living on a boat. It was just not the right move for us. I had to be realistic and bankruptcy had made me hunker down again.

73

Sebring, Restaurant Critic

This had to be our forever home. At first, just adjusting to the newness of it all was cool. Where to put our furniture, what was the best place for our special black leather *Eames* chair, what about adding a stainless pot rack in the kitchen, and where to stack all my white dishes and treasures.

Mike said, "There's a Harley dealership up the highway, I'm just going to look." I encouraged him saying, "I know it is your special thing to have a motorcycle again." So before long, we had a shiny, new, yellow 1200 Sportster in our new garage.

I had a bit of time on my hands, ha! What a new concept.

I perused the Sebring Highlands Today newspaper. My culinary credentials promoted a thought that maybe I could be an anonymous food critic for the local scene, slyly testing the ambiance and menus in this region. Using the motorcycle might add a twist to my reviews. The editor admitted it could be a good thing.

He said, "They had thought about having a critic before but never had a qualified subject." So before too many days passed, I was Ms. Cuisine, the anonymous, opinionated food sleuth. Where to begin?

Sebring has a famous state park with a rustic restaurant within, so here is a record of my first weekly column.

Ms. Cuisine

Ms. Cuisine has an opinion.

Hammock Inn Offers Great Ambiance

Like the teddy bear picnic song, you're in for a big surprise. Hammock State Park is right off Highway 27 in Sebring and inside the park is the Hammock Inn Restaurant. It does cost $4.00 to enjoy the park, but if you are just going to the restaurant there is no charge.

You'll be intrigued with the restaurant's wooded and rustic setting. A pleasant deep aroma of home-smoked meats filled the sitting area. On weekends from 8-10 a.m. breakfasts of eggs, sausages and beverages are served to motorcyclers, campers and drive-ins alike for a mere $5.50 all you can eat. Tuesday through Sunday the kitchen is open for lunch and dinner, closed on Monday.

If the weather is especially crisp, the big stone fireplace is set ablaze with a crackling real wood fire.

On our noon visit, we tested tomato/basil bisque, soup of the day, hand battered fish and chips with coleslaw. My soup was very much a step above Campbell's and the large beer battered fish was crusty and delicious. My companion chose a traditional cheese burger, but it was very nicely served and cooked just right, not dry. Lemon sodas rounded out the day although I was interested in the wild orange pie and ice cream of the same flavor. Wild oranges, a catchy description, were on the property originally, but it is now illegal to pick them, so the current restaurant owner has her own version of this recipe. Desserts are all housemade and whole pies are $13.50. Prices are low and reasonable and this is a different destination for lunch.

Take a drive into Hammock State Park and be surprised at what you will find going on in the woods today.

This adventure as an undercover agent continued for many months until one restaurant owner was affronted to know Ms. Cuisine didn't like his steaks, wait staff or the quality delivered at his long time establishment. Much inner turmoil erupted at the editor's desk. It had been fun and challenging, helping some restaurants with positive reviews or mixed constructive feedback with suggestions to others. When the conflict with the steak house ensued, the editor caved in. I had really stirred things up. What he really needed was just someone to tell people where each place was located and a list of their food, not a real critic. I tactfully withdrew and threw in the towel. Sebring was not ready for Prime Time.

"What should I do now," Julia Child once queried when she landed in France. It was the same for me. Projects in Sebring just seem to evolve! Requests for birthday cakes, food for small groups and getting acquainted with new friends in our park filled each day. South Florida College phoned and thought it would be a good idea if I gave a few classes during the winter season. So I did that. I was supposed to be retired but it was still fun. I gathered together an eight week series that highlighted the Florida theme.

74
Special Visitors, Wes and David

My thoughts floated back in time to when Anton had died. My neighbors in West Van, Wesley and David, stepped in to strengthen our friendship. They had loved my school and seemed to admire all that I did. Wesley was the chef of the two and absorbed all the current trendy food ideas and cooked quite a lot.

Remembering fun times…late in the evening, when I needed tasters for a new dessert creation, I would phone next door. "Are you guys home for the night? Come over for dessert." They would come over about eleven P.M. That particular time it was Floating Island, (Oeufs à la Neige), a delicious concoction of custard and meringue with a caramel, sugar cage threaded like a dome over the top or simply drizzled over the meringue. Quite spectacular!

We all laughed thinking how funny this scene looked to anyone able to view the three of us spooning up the velvety sauce with bits of meringue, picking up caramel threads from the superimposed dome with our fingers and savoring the flavors like children. We all decided it was really good. This recipe should be included in a class.

OEUFS À LA NEIGE AUX PÉTALS

Here is the recipe that Wesley, David and I taste tested one late evening. This is a very French dessert also known in English as Floating Island. Originally it was simple: a childish custard, but the special caramel cage over top lifts it to a sophisticated height. It can be created as an option or just drape threads of caramel over surface. (Also add rose petals).

Medium

Custard
10 cups milk, hot
12 eggs, yolks and whites separated
¾ cup sugar
4 tsp. rose water flavouring

Method
Beat ¾ cups sugar with yolks.
Whisk in hot milk from above, strain back into saucepan, add rose scented rose water, cook to make a light custard, strain. Cool.

Method for Meringues
Whisk above egg whites stiff, adding 4 Tbsp. rose scented sugar.
Over simmering water, using a large dessert spoon, scoop whites and poach egg whites, turning once. Set aside onto platter.

Float one prepared Oeuf in shallow single serving dessert dish on a pool of custard. Decorate plate and decorate meringue with candied rose petals if available from an organic or non-sprayed rose bush.

(Optional)
Cook 1 cup granulated sugar with ¼ cup water to hard crack stage, with a drop of lemon juice to dark caramel color. It will thread when drawing a fork through and up, lifting from the pot to harden immediately.
Thread over finished dessert or use to make a dome and serve.
(1 cup sugar layered with rose petals for flavor).

Note
When I did this dessert in white Sulphur Springs Napa, for Cal Berkley, I needed rose petals for great effect. Because it was August, roses were in full bloom. My problem was, these gardens were not mine. I found a suitable bush, went up to the door and said, "I am a chef doing this special thing for UC Berkley here in St. Helena and need some of your perfect petals from the bush in your backyard." I'm sure she thought it was weird but gave me a basket full of petals and I was on my way.

When I first moved to San Francisco, Wes and David kept in touch, and visited me several times while I got used to being on my own. They made me feel so special and said, "You're doing a great job," reassuring me that I would be okay.

My fabulous stove and house in West Vancouver was past history but the fact that my current, single, rented room didn't even have a bath tub was sort of a joke. We three had been out for dinner when they said, "Come back to our room for late night drinks. We're staying in a boutique hotel in the S. F. Opera district. Come and use our deep bath tub." How weird was that but it was just what I needed.

Before midnight, there I was luxuriating in silky warm water up to my neck, enjoying their English bath soaps while opera music wafts in from their bed-sitting room. Later, as I departed the empty lobby at one A.M., it had an odd feel. I hurried out into the darkness, handed my ticket to the valet, gave him a good tip and drove off in my van feeling like a painted lady of the night.

Forward to 1996 when Mike and I visited Vancouver so my children and friends could meet my beau and approve of my choice, wedding talk began. When we suggested a September affair, Wes and David stepped in to host the pre-wedding rehearsal dinner, and offered to have this party at their beautiful Vancouver home. Elaborate invitations went out announcing a 'Soirée' in our honor. Forward in time to Florida; I received a newsy letter from Wesley, with the thought that we should try to get together while they were planning a holiday in southern Florida, Ft. Lauderdale. It would be a nostalgia trip through time for them. They had stayed at a funky motel by the sea and fondly remember the wonderful time they had there. That was twenty-five years ago and they still remain a couple. They were seeking to reflect on their lives to this point.

"How far away from Ft. Lauderdale were we, in Sebring?" they asked.

I set up a day and time that fit into their schedule, with them coming to our house in Sebring for lunch. It had been quite a few years since we had seen each other. I was excited.

They arrived in a trendy Mini Cooper car and appeared just as young as the last time we had seen each other: always full of energy and bearing unusual gifts. They loved our new home and took some fabulous photos that I received some weeks later. Wesley's artistic genius with a camera captured our house making it appear like a shoot in a 'Luxury Homes Magazine.' Wow!

As we ate, each reminisce became a full blown story jogging my memory as told from their point of view. For many of my catered events, they remembered every hilarious detail hearing our hustle and bustle from over the hedge, and my vivid stories relayed later. The evening at the Vancouver Aquarium when all the electrical plugs blew, when a dumped tray of hors d'oeuvres was reassembled from the back of the truck, or the dessert was almost late but arrived on time, or my assistant, Joanne, rushed to get to the party, stepped in a sink hole in the lawn, her catering uniform now mud up to her knees. All these possible disasters were somehow averted by my devoted staff.

Wes and David are real friends, so special. They influenced my life in countless ways. I can only be grateful for their continued presence throughout the years.

75

Retirement

We now live frugally: after all, we have what we need. Declaring bankruptcy was a blow but I know there will still be wonderful times ahead. We will manage, I have survived again. Mike, Gracie and I have found our sunny Nirvana here in Sebring, Florida. (Gracie, a fluffy Bearded Collie, is our newest rescue after dear Muffin died last year).

I think my children are proud of me that I have stayed productive and strong all these years.

I have to accept that I am aging, even though I try to hold onto youthful things. I swim, play Pickle-Ball, and we still ride motorcycles. The years are slipping by. My life's arc is on the downward curve. When I walk our Gracie in the morning, I take time to do an overhead Yoga stretch, look up at the blue sky and thank my angels for all my blessings. I have time to bake for friends, read a new best seller or make sure the birthday cards are sent on time with a newsy note inside. The many roles of my life have come full circle: I'm the one to make the phone calls or send e-mails instead of waiting to hear from them, my children and grandchildren.

Ten of my Pickleball friends here in Tanglewood had recently motorcycled to an interesting Florida destination that had a Caramel Walnut Pie on their lunch menu.

They said, "We need to know how to make that, it was so good." and somebody piped up with, "Barbara is a pastry chef, let's get her to show us how." A few weeks later, the date was arranged and they all came over to my kitchen at 3 PM for a fun class on how to make the pastry, the filling and what the oven temperature should be. I had two pies made ahead and we made one in the class. While the fresh pie was baking, Mike kept everyone's attention as he demonstrated how to produce crispy pizzas in short order out on the grill. It was a wonderful, impromptu afternoon, filled with some serious techniques regarding the pie pastry and lots of laughs between the beer and fabulous pizza. The pies were cut and we all indulged in the rich filling and flaky pastry. The next day and for weeks afterward, Pizza and Walnut Pie was the topic of interest at the courts. Many accolades and sincere notes came my way from that little get together. The opportunity to impart my baking skills and know-how to my Pickleball friends, gave me a wonderful warm feeling, confirming I had added something of value to their lives.

PIZZA FROM THE GRILL

These delicious pizzas are easy to make and with a few ahead of time preparations, they come together quickly. The recipe makes 4, 12" pizzas

Dough
1 cup warm water
1 Tbsp. sugar
1 pkg. (1½ oz.) active dry yeast

2½ cups all-purpose flour
1 cup cake flour
1 Tbsp. Kosher salt

Add
2 Tbsp. olive oil

Method
Combine water, sugar and yeast, let proof 5 minutes.
Mix flours and salt in processor, or standing mixer, fitted with dough hook. Add oil to yeast mixture once it has turned foamy and is proofed, then add to flour in bowl.
Knead on low speed 10 minutes or if kneading by hand about the same time.
Place dough in lightly oiled bowl, turning to coat, dough and cover with plastic wrap.
Set in a warm place, (I like to use a slightly warmed oven), let rise about 2 hours until double.
Punch down and divide into 4 balls, pinching to close cut area.
Cover and let rise 1 more hour.
While dough is rising, assemble special tomato sauce and toppings.

Oven Roasted Tomato Sauce
4 lb. Roma tomatoes, quartered
1 yellow onion, chopped
4 cloves garlic, whole
2 tsp. Kosher salt
1 tsp. red pepper flakes
1 tsp. sugar
¼ cup olive oil

Method
Pre- heat oven to 450
Put all ingredients on 2 sheet pans and roast about 40 minutes.
Remove from oven and mash lightly, leaving quite chunky.
Cool
Stir in 1 bunch of chiffonade of fresh basil.

Toppings
Pepperoni- tomato sauce, fresh mozzarella, sliced pepperoni, parmesan cheese.

Mediterranean- tomato sauce, cubed Fontina cheese, small slices of salami or sausage, Kalamata olives, fresh basil, parmesan.

All Cheese- tomato sauce, mozzarella, pepper-jack, parmesan, goat cheese, a chiffonade of fresh sage.

Method and Shaping Dough
Roll-out dough circles to about 12 inches. Irregular shape is fine.
Have grill hot!

Place dough circles on sheet pan beside grill station.
Separate each circle with parchment. (Prevents sticking together)
Place first circle on grill, close lid, let bake about 2 minutes until puffed and bubbled.
Flip over, brush surface with olive oil.
Add light layer of tomato sauce, then toppings of choice. Not too much filling.
Cook 4-5 minutes until cheese melts. Edges will burn slightly.
Slide onto pizza pan or back of a sheet pan, carry to kitchen and cut. Enjoy!

SALTED CARAMEL WALNUT PIE

<u>Easy</u>

<u>Crust</u>
⅓ cup chilled unsalted butter, (part Crisco)
1 cup flour
1Tbsp. powdered sugar
1Tbsp. apple cider vinegar
Pinch salt
2 or more Tbsp. ice water

<u>Method</u>
Place butter, Crisco, salt and flour in processor, whirl to just mix butter to pea size.
Add vinegar and water through feed tube.
Press on-off just to bring it slightly together.
Turn out on counter, press together.
Wrap in plastic, chill ½ hour.
Rollout on flour dusted counter to 12 inch circle.
Place in lightly greased 9 inch pie pan, prick the bottom with a fork and chill or freeze dough while making filling.

Filling
1 cup brown sugar
¼ cup white sugar
½ tsp. fine sea salt
½ cup butter, melted
¼ cup boiling water
4 eggs, beaten
1Tbsp. milk
1½ Tbsp. vanilla and ⅛ cup Bourbon or Applejack cognac
2 cups toasted walnuts, roughly chopped

I Tbsp. coarse sea salt
Purchased caramel dessert sauce.

Filling and Baking

Preheat oven to 400
Mix brown sugar and white sugar, salt and melted butter. Add boiling water. Stir until sugar dissolves.
Add the beaten egg and milk. Add bourbon and vanilla.
Mix in half of the walnuts to filling.
Remove pie crust from freezer and spread about ½ cup caramel dessert sauce over bottom of crust.
Sprinkle rest of walnuts over caramel. (This way the walnuts are more evenly distributed.)
Pour filling into crust.
Bake in lower⅓ of oven, at 400 for 10 minutes, then reduce down to 350 for at least 30 minutes more or until nicely browned.

Sprinkle coarse sea salt over pie
Cool pie on rack at least 2 hours. (Optional, drizzle more caramel sauce over top of pie.)

Serve with vanilla ice cream or real whipped cream.

76
Florida Baking

Today my kitchen is set up for a morning of baking. The recipe and all the ingredients are on the counter for easy assembly. I have six small muffin tins and prepare to bake a Florida specialty, cupcakes with fresh Coconut. Cupcakes have had quite resurgence these past years and bakers have created new flavors and icings. There are trendy mini bakery stores that have popped up all over the country that sell only cupcakes. Amazing!

BARBARA'S COCONUT CUPCAKES, FRESH COCONUT AND SEVEN -MINUTE FROSTING

Notes, about fresh Coconuts. They are easy to crack. First pierce two of the three eyes with a skewer. Pour out the milk and save. Place whole coconut in a 350 oven on a sheet pan for 10 minutes. Coconut will crack. Pry out the meat and use a peeler to remove any brown skin. Shred meat and use or freeze.

Barbara J Miachika

Easy
1¼ cups all-purpose flour
2 tsp. baking powder
½ tsp. salt
½ cup packed sweetened shredded coconut
1½ sticks unsalted butter, softened
1⅓ cups sugar
2 large eggs plus 2 egg whites
¾ cup unsweetened coconut milk
1 tsp. vanilla
1½ cups unsweetened flake coconut
Extra flaked, fresh coconut and sugared, sliced almonds for décor

Method
Preheat oven 350
Line standard muffin cups with paper liners or use foil liners on sheet pan.
Whisk dry ingredients in a bowl, adding sweetened coconut to dry ingredients.
Cream butter, sugar until fluffy and well blended.
Add eggs, 1 at a time.
Reduce mixer speed; add any other wet ingredients, vanilla and coconut milk.
Add flour to butter mixture, alternating with wet, ending with dry.
Divide batter among cups about ⅔ full. Leave room for high top icing.

Make Frosting
1½ cups plus 2 Tbsp. sugar
⅔ cup water
2Tbsp. light corn syrup

6 egg whites
Fresh grated coconut
Sugared almond slices

Method

Mix 1½ cups sugar, water and light corn syrup in small saucepan over medium high heat until sugar is dissolved, cooking on high for about 2 minutes or to 230 on a candy thermometer.
Meanwhile, in a stand mixer, whisk whites on medium speed to soft peaks.
With mixer running, add the last 2 Tbsp. sugar.
With mixer on medium low, pour hot sugar in steady stream down side of bowl; now whisking on high until stiff and glossy peaks (about 7 minutes).

Use to ice cupcakes, adding <u>fresh</u> grated coconut flakes and sugared almond slices over top.

*Sugared sliced Almonds- 1 egg white, sliced almonds, and sugar; toss together, spread out on sheet pan, toast in oven to golden brown and crispy.

77

Classes

Six A.M., barely light, and it promised to be another perfect morning in Florida. I dressed quickly, grabbed a sip of espresso and was out the door with Gracie for her first walk of the day. She barked her happiness and ran along in her Beardie bouncy style to greet her other doggie friends: she sat at the appropriate signal hoping to get a cookie. The routine never changes. As I walked, the air that swirled over me was delicious at this early hour, so silky and smooth.

Back home, Gracie patrolled her dish for treats while I put out breakfast for Mike. Next, I changed into my sports clothes and arrived at the Pickleball courts in time for an hour of intense play. "What a great work out, so much better than going to the gym!"

I was home by nine, sweaty but maybe one pound lighter. Showered and ready for whatever might be on my calendar today, the phone interrupted my thoughts…

I said, "Hello,"

A voice said, "This is South Florida Community College. We wonder if you might give a few more cooking classes"…

END

Index

Coeur à la Crème-79
Hot Lemon Soufflés-75
Cream Plaschinke, (Yugoslavian Crepes)-117
Perfect Chocolate Mousse-131
Frozen Soufflé à l'Orange-154
Apple Strudel-206
Barbara's House Truffles-288
Raspberry Meringues-235
Mango Mousse Ring-242
Blueberry/Lemon Crisp-224
Apple/Cranberry Crisp-225
Mark Hopkins Double Chocolate Dome-295
Jean Pierre's Pear Clafoutis/Honey-315
Simple Crème Caramel/Vodka Berries-53
Barbara's Nouvelle Crème Brûlée-8
Baked Alaska-XX11

Cakes
Aunt Faye's Christmas Cake-273
Gateau Elegant au Citron-348
Boudina, Mini Molten Chocolate Cakes-308
Master Wedding Cake 1, Anthony and Victoria,-165, 2-Paul and Julie-193
LeNôtre Concord Gateau-173
Death by Chocolate Log-145
Flo Braker's Fraisia, Strawberry Dome Cake-149
Best Ever Chocolate Sheet Cake-38
Chocolate Chantilly Cake with Fans-177
Barbara's New York Cheesecake-68
Lemon Poppy Seed Pound Cake-4

Orange Roll/Tea and Grand Marnier-49
Chocolat Almond Torta-25
Boston Cream Pie, (Cake)-227
His Highness Gateau, (White Chocolate)-214
Les Caneles, Bordeaux Mini Cakes-317
Chocolate Cloud Cake in a Forest-364
Chocolate Imperialé Flourless Cake-20
Orange Bavarian Torte-258

Cookies, Scones, Muffins
Barbara's Coconut Cupcakes/Seven Minute Frosting, 397
Nanaimo Bars, Canadian Sweet-268
Large Chocolate Tuiles, Cookies 94
Caramel/Pecan Chocolate Bars-124
Crystalized Ginger Sables, English Shortbread Cookies-216
Biscotti, Original-243
Biscotti, Barbara's-245
Mike's Corn Meal Scones/Blueberries-368
Basic Sourdough Bread/Starter and Bread-43
Cranberry/Orange Muffins 370
Corn Mini Jalepeños Muffins-283
Sugared Almonds-399

Pies, Tarts
Apple/Yogurt Breakfast Tarts-222
Barbara's American Apple Pie, Crumble Topping-34
Meringue Angel Pie-31
Rhubarb Butter Tarts-262
Salted Caramel Walnut Pie-394
Chez Panisse's Basic Pastry-315

Ice Cream
Lime/Rum Ice Cream-237
Prune Ice Cream-218
Gelato Spazzacamino, Marcella Hazan-157

For more about Barbara
go to

email, miachikab@yahoo.com
www.ndygirls.com

Made in the USA
San Bernardino, CA
01 March 2014